University of
Washington

THE CAMPUS GUIDE

# University of Washington

Norman J. Johnston
Photographs by Jay Dotson
Foreword by Richard L. McCormick

**Princeton Architectural Press**
*NEW YORK* | *2001*

This book is dedicated to the late Charles E. Odegaard (1911–1999), president of the University of Washington from 1958 to his retirement in 1973, whose commitment to the campus and its development accounts for many of the achievements that this book records.

This book has been made possible through the generous support of the Graham Foundation for Advanced Studies in the Fine Arts.

Princeton Architectural Press
37 East 7th Street
New York, NY 10003
212.995.9620

For a free catalog of other books published by Princeton Architectural Press, call toll free 1.800.722.6657 or visit our web site at www.papress.com

Editing: Jan Cigliano
Copyediting: Heather Ewing
Design: Sara E. Stemen
Layout: Mary-Neal Meador
Maps: Jane Garvie
Special thanks to Ann Alter, Amanda Atkins, Nicola Bednarek, Eugenia Bell, Caroline Green, Beth Harrison, Mia Ihara, Clare Jacobson, Leslie Ann Kent, Mark Lamster, Anne Nitschke, Lottchen Shivers, Jennifer Thompson, and Deb Wood of Princeton Architectural Press
—Kevin C. Lippert, *publisher*

Library of Congress Cataloguing-in-Publication Data
Johnston, Norman J.
    University of Washington / Norman J. Johnston ; photographs by Jay Dotson ; foreword by Richard L. McCormick.
        p. cm. — (The campus guide)
    Includes bibliographical references and index.
    ISBN 1-56898-247-X
    1. University of Washington—Guidebooks.    2. University of Washington—Pictorial works.    I. Title.    II. Campus guide (New York, N.Y.)

LD5754.J58   2001
378.797'772—dc21                                                                                    00-044606
                                                                                                          CIP

Printed and bound in China

05 04 03 02 01   5 4 3 2 1  First Edition

# How to use this book

This Guide is intended for all those—visitors, alumni, and daily users of the campus alike—who would like to know something of the history of the University of Washington's campus and that of the buildings which occupy it, of the reasons for their existence and character, and something of the relationship through history of the university to the city of Seattle. It includes material on the University's notable historic and contemporary buildings and the impact that various events, individuals, and university administrations have had on the campus and its development. The text discusses how and why new and old come together to define the campus and especially the way in which the University came endowed with a plan of dramatic dimensions, which largely accounts for what one finds on the campus today.

After an overall introduction that notes the original downtown campus and the move in 1895 to the present location, the book is then divided into eleven Walks covering the major campus areas. Each Walk is a separate chapter comprised of an introduction that describes any unique circumstances of history, plan, topography, and the like, with a birds-eye view drawing identifying each building on the Walk, followed by entries on each individual building or building cluster. A photograph of the building and basic information on dates and designers accompany most entries.

Classroom buildings and open spaces on campus are open during daylight hours, though visitors are asked to show consideration of classes and other university activities.

University Bookstore, University Way (206.634.3400), with branch stores in the Student Union Building (206.543.5986) and the South Campus Center (206.543.6582). There is also a downtown branch at 1201 Fourth Avenue (206.545.9230).

Further Information from:
Visitors Information Center
4014 University Way Northeast
Seattle, Washington 98195
206.543.9198
E-mail: uwvic@u.washington.edu
www.u.washington.edu

# Foreword

*Science Quad and Drumheller Fountain*

University campuses are living monuments to the generations of people who have come before and who helped shape the campus we see today, whether they were students, faculty, or staff, architects, builders, landscape designers, or urban planners. It would be impossible to pay appropriate tribute to everyone who made this splendid campus what it is—a sylvan oasis in the heart of one of this country's greatest cities and one of its most beautiful and naturally endowed settings for a university campus. On two sides, the campus rests on the shores of Lake Washington and Portage Bay. On clear days, sunrise and sunset illuminate the two mountain ranges that cradle Seattle, the Cascades to the east and the Olympic Mountains to the west. Dominating the horizon in one direction is the majestic Mount Rainier.

It is a symbol of the care with which generations of campus developers nurtured the relationship to these natural wonders that a single vista defines the core of the campus and has become its hallmark: the long stretch of open landscape, framed by a number of imposing buildings, we call Rainier Vista. It was established as a predominant feature of the campus in preparation for the 1909 Alaska-Yukon-Pacific Exposition, held on the grounds of the slowly developing campus. It has remained a signature feature ever since.

Those of us who have been entrusted with this beautiful campus through the years have, with few exceptions, taken great care to carry on the legacy of its early planners. The University of Washington is one of America's finest public universities, and throughout the course of its history, it has had to make massive investments in the physical spaces in which teachers, scientists, scholars, and artists can accomplish their best and most creative work. By far the majority of these investments were made by the citizens of the state of Washington—through their elected leaders—who time and time again recognized the value such contributions brought to the state and the individuals who study here. In recent years, this investment in the state has been augmented by gifts from philanthropic friends of the university. The benefits to the campus have been significant.

Careful attention to campus architecture continues as we modernize our facilities and expand our capabilities to work at the frontiers of knowledge. If you spend some time with this book enjoying the various Walks on campus, I think you will see the care I am describing. As we

*Statue of Washington with Olympic Mountains*

develop the campus to the west, we are continuing the tradition of thought-ful planning, sensitive architecture, and a respect for the importance of open space to the living and learning environment we create for students.

No one is more qualified to write about this campus and its build-ings than the author of this guide, Norman J. Johnston. For decades a dedi-cated and beloved professor of architecture and a historian of the campus, Professor Johnston brings to this guide a wealth of knowledge about the campus's past, a deep veneration for the men and women who made it what it is, and an abiding passion for all it can offer to inquiring minds. On behalf of all of us—past, present, and future—at the University of Washington, I want to express my gratitude to Professor Johnston for undertaking this labor of love.

*Richard L. McCormick*
*President*
*University of Washington*

The University of Washington, the first such public institution to be established on the Pacific Coast, was the product of Washington pioneer initiative emerging out of the most unpromising circumstances. Seattle, founded in 1851, was still only a village ten years later, consisting of some 302 souls (Indians not included) housed in a cluster of wood-frame construction, facing muddy streets on the shores and recently logged-off slopes above Puget Sound's Elliott Bay. This village could not even claim either a public grade school or high school!

Yet within the territorial leadership of that early date there were those with a vision, especially the first territorial governor, Isaac I. Stevens, and the Rev. Daniel Bagley. It was the former who pointed out the assistance the federal government offered for education, especially through dedicated land grant income from timber harvests. But it was Bagley, only a recent resident in 1860, who inspired local ambitions with the enthusiasm of a town promoter. Seattle, typical of America's mid-century western urban expansion, was on the hunt for that unique distinction sure to inspire its prosperous future and lure new residents eager to share in it. Public institutions such as state capitals, county seats, penitentiaries, and asylums were especially favored as such lure; Bagley, with both economic and intellectual motives, proposed a university to grace Seattle's future.

Such thinking was not an exceptional phenomenon for its day; by 1860 thirteen states had already established state universities west of the Appalachian Mountains, receiving timbered land grants from Congress for their support. The Territory of Washington joined them when—with the astute political guidance of Bagley, now teamed with Arthur A. and Mary Denny (among Seattle's leading founders)—the legislative bill was passed in 1861 declaring that the University of Washington would be "located and established" at Seattle. The villagers had indeed managed a coup whose many-faceted benefits are a continuing blessing: "The University of a Thousand Years."

That bill also authorized the finding of a ten-acre site for the university and its "clearing and improving." Because of the somewhat open-ended nature of the bill's language—abetted by the willingness of Bagley (one of the three commissioners granted the powers to act in the university's behalf) to interpret it generously—in remarkably short order Bagley had been chosen president of its board of regents, the university had its ten-acre site, clearance took place, and on May 20, 1861, the cornerstone of its building was laid.

Processes had surely been eased by the Denny's support, for it was he who not only donated the bulk of the required site but enticed Charles and Mary Terry and Edward Lander to join him in meeting the ten-acre requirement. At the time the site, Denny's Knoll, was uptown literally as well

*Downtown University, 1870s*

as figuratively. It sloped both southwest toward Elliott Bay, toward distant views of Puget Sound and the Olympics, and south toward the developed part of town. And there for the next thirty-five years the university was to remain, its site dominated by the pleasant classical dignity of its building, the only one in local contemporary photographs demonstrating much in the way of architectural pretensions.

By the late 1880s Seattle was no longer a village but, rather, a respectable town of 40,000; the relative isolation of the university campus had disappeared. Creeping development now surrounded its site. Although this development was mostly residential, enough less salubrious construction and influences had drifted uptown to cause the regents concern for the students' spiritual welfare. The physical plant of the university—which encompassed two residences, a dormitory, an armory hall, a "lodging," and a henhouse—was by then notorious for its deterioration and neglect. As the college enrollments neared 300 people, the regents recognized the size and condition limitations of the present situation. Clearly, ten acres were no longer sufficient, but the existing development prevented contiguous campus expansion. A special legislative committee established to examine the situation and suggest possible alternatives agreed; in 1889 it reported, "The grounds of the university in the city of Seattle are in a pitiably neglected and forlorn condition, and have been so for years. An old ramshackle fence surrounds them, and often in places knocked down or blown down, cows invade and trespass." Clearly, the time had come for more ambitious thinking about the university's future.

The late 1880s were a propitious time for such thinking. In November 1889, the Territory of Washington became a state. And, whereas the Territorial Legislature had been tight-fisted in its financial policy toward the university, the State Legislature proved to be friendlier. Not only was it more supportive of the university's immediate needs, but—more significantly—

it was appreciative of the potential for the future, not only that of the university itself but for the state as well. Here was a rekindling of Daniel Bagley's vision.

The 1890 legislature provided further momentum, the launch pad for dramatic action: "Ampler grounds are essential to the property and well-being of the university, and grounds more remote from the center of a rapidly growing and expanding city . . . [the campus] is best removed from the excitements and temptations incident to city life and environments." The report concluded that authority be granted to sell the present campus and seek a new one of at least forty acres, "conveniently near the city." Later, further selection specifications were that the site be within six miles of the present campus and its minimum size was increased to one hundred acres.

A new and major figure was introduced into the act: the six-foot-six-inch Edmond S. Meany. An 1885 UW graduate, a journalist and a promoter, Meany soon joined the ranks of Daniel Bagley and Arthur and Mary Denny in the importance of their impact on the history of the institution. His election to the new state legislature was based on a campaign that championed the interests of his alma mater. Propitiously, his subsequent appointments in that body as chairman of the House University committee and thereafter chairman of the legislative joint committee created "to find, acquire, and guide a new campus" provided him with splendid opportunities to advance those interests.

Site selection proceeded apace. Of the several options considered by the committee, one on Lake Washington known as "Interlaken" met all the technical requirements. Additionally, it appealed for its waterfront location, its views of the city and lakes and distant mountains, and its generous undeveloped and available acreage. Initially the committee settled for an acquisition of only 160 of the available 580-acre site, though Meany, biding his time, aimed for the full acreage. As events developed, he would get it. Uncertain national and local economics, the failure to sell the downtown campus, excessive cost estimates for overly ambitious initial site planning and construction, and legal challenges for construction funding all militated against early progress. Meany used the time well, however, crafting a new bill that the legislature passed, authorizing purchase of the full site backed by a $150,000 appropriation for construction, and allowing the university regents to proceed with development of the new campus. On March 3, 1894, Governor McGraw signed Meany's bill and the university turned its full attention to bringing to fruition the promise of its new site.

It can't be emphasized too much the "luck of the draw" the university experienced as it moved toward the planning, design, and construction of its new campus. There was the magic of the site itself, with its location near to the central city but sufficiently removed to create its own and generously scaled new unique world. Then there was the general ambiance surrounding it, an almost 360-degree sweep of vistas, reaching west to the Olympics and

Lake Union, south to Portage Bay, east to Lake Washington and the distant Cascades, and southeast to Mount Rainier. What other campus could possibly enjoy such a sweep of natural beauty? The wonder is that to a remarkable extent all this promise was through the years substantially realized—but not immediately: that was where chance worked for the university, not against it.

Although beginnings were pedestrian enough, the design of the initial building was quite compelling. In contrast to the many red brick "Old Mains" on campuses scattered about the country in the latter half of the nineteenth century, the university's first building on its new campus was of respectable stone in a variation of French Renaissance style, which has stood well the test of time and taste. Its siting was haphazard, however, if one accepts the probably apocryphal story of its selection: a member of the board of regents involved in the planning, weary with tramping over the rough-shorn landscape of the campus, declared as he probed his umbrella into a rotten log, "I don't know about you fellows but I say, put it here!" Regardless, Denny Hall was built, and the university made its official move from downtown Seattle to its new campus by occupying it in 1895.

The location of the subsequent men's and women's dorms and other minor structures received no more adequate siting attention. There must, however, have been uneasiness amongst the regents with such ad hoc handling of campus development, for the board turned at this time to a professor in the engineering college, A. H. Fuller. They charged him with the task of developing a plan that would encompass existing construction and provide some sense of location for future building. His efforts resulted in 1898 in what is known as the Oval Plan, of no notable distinction except that it officially sanctioned a plan with a southwest-northeast orientation and established for the three major university buildings their roles in it. But it

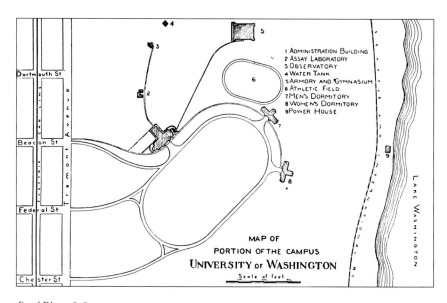

*Oval Plan, 1898*

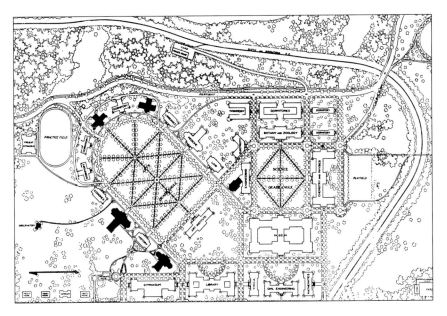

*Olmsted Plan, 1904*

encompassed only the upper third or so of the acreage the board had pur-
chased. What of the rest of the site?

Somewhere in the workings of the board of regents lingered
perhaps a skepticism about the Oval Plan; didn't the university deserve
more? That could explain why the regents turned to what was then the pre-
eminent landscape planning firm in the country, the Olmsted Brothers of
Brookline, Massachusetts. Frederick Law Olmsted, designer of New York's
Central Park, had founded the firm. The Olmsteds' price was right—one
thousand dollars plus expenses, for a comprehensive plan which in due
course under the guidance of John C. Olmsted the firm delivered to the
board in 1904. It took into account the orientation established by the Oval
Plan, extending it to incorporate the bulk of campus acreage, at least within
the sweep of the railroad track that determined much of the campus limits
to the south and east.

A self-enclosed scheme, the plan filled campus space with a rigid
geometry in which buildings were located almost haphazardly. Beyond a
somewhat casual grouping of the Arts Quadrangle to the north and Science
Quadrangle to the south (terminology and associations which remain to this
day) there is a puzzling irrationality of placement. The gymnasium is remote
from the playing field and practice field; an enormous museum is buried
within the campus, rather than sited for easy access by the public and students; dormitories are hidden away among the sciences. The plan entirely
failed to respond to the brilliant potentials of the site beyond its legal perimeter. Surely, had that plan been followed, the university would have been adequately served. But the site's potential would have been ignored, remaining
only a typical public university with a plan of no environmental distinction.

Again, circumstances intervened and the university escaped that fate. In 1906 Seattle business interests, inspired by world's fairs such as had occurred in Chicago, St. Louis, and—closer to home—Portland, Oregon, joined in this national enthusiasm. Seattle's fair, intended to demonstrate to the world the achievements of American life, industry, and the sponsoring city, was to be known as the Alaska-Yukon-Pacific Exposition (AYPE). As the organizers searched for a site, their attention naturally turned to the largely undeveloped university campus. What better arrangement than to come to an agreement with the regents for the AYPE to occupy the lower and undeveloped two-thirds of the campus for its purposes? The AYPE would establish an appropriate site plan with a circulation and open space system, build both permanent and temporary buildings, landscape the site, and, once the fair was over, remove temporary construction and turn the campus back to the regents. The regents in turn would then have a campus plan realized on the ground, with several buildings left for university purposes—no paper plan but one with an achieved design framework which over the years would be filled in by the university's own permanent construction. The regents accepted the proposal and were given yet another chance to enjoy fully the promise of the Interlake site.

This time the Olmsteds got it right. Perhaps when John C. Olmsted visited the campus in preparation of the firm's 1914 campus plan it was an overcast day, cutting him off from any sign of the regional vistas surrounding the campus. Surely, their 1904 plan gave no thought to that reality. But on his return in 1906 had the sun shown, the sky opened, the horizons been clear? The Olmsted 1909 AYPE plan fully exploited the site's prospects. The plan's overall orientation was to the southeast, its axes and vistas and open spaces defined by the fair's permanent and temporary construction. The plan's vistas drew the distant mountain ranges, the lakes, and most of all the monumental nobility of Mount Rainier into the scheme, campus and environment marrying in a visually dramatic work-

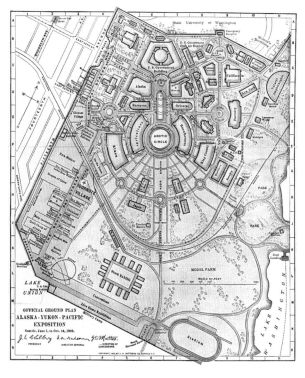

*Plan of Alaska-Yukon-Pacific Exposition, 1909*

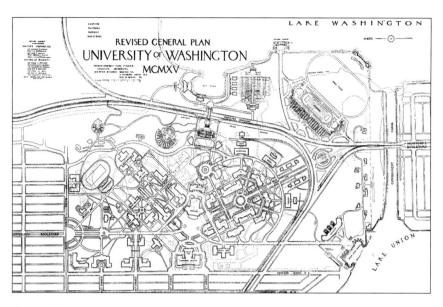

*Regents Plan, 1915*

ing relationship. The fair was a great success (it even turned a profit); with
the campus returned to the university, the opportunity and challenge were to
honor suitably the plan that it had inherited.

The regents' first step in that effort focused first on bringing about
a harmonious union between the now grandly developed plan of the lower
two thirds of the campus where the AYPE had been and the neglected upper
third of the campus where the university's original buildings were located.
Toward that end, the regents turned once again to the Olmsted Brothers.
Their resulting proposal was a curiously inharmonious plan, unhappily meld-
ing the monumental classicism of the fair with a kind of irregular romanti-
cism to the north, as featured in some of the firm's environmental planning
elsewhere. The regents dismissed the firm and turned instead to the local
architect Carl F. Gould. A man well couched in terms of the principles of
Beaux-Arts design, he was to play an increasingly substantial role in the
development of the campus in the years ahead. The regents charged Gould
to succeed where the Olmsteds had failed. The result was the 1915 "Revised
General Plan of the University of Washington," commonly known as the
Regents Plan. The plan dictated that all future construction would be in the
Collegiate Gothic style, a design proviso to which university policy adhered,
at least in upper campus, until the 1950s. The plan has subsequently undergone further study and revisions, but, remarkably, the spirit of the 1915 design
has been continuously honored—its vistas, spaces, and grouping of functions,
buildings, and landscaping—mitigating the impact of development that the
campus has undergone in the plan's eighty-five-year history.

Examining the Regents Plan you find two fundamental elements that
explain its pattern. First, there are planned open spaces of varying degrees of

prominence. Some, such as the Liberal Arts Quad or Hub Yard, are extensive in scale and importance, whereas others are more private, subdued, and secluded, such as Sylvan Theater or Grieg Garden for example. These planned open spaces play a vital, almost sacred role in campus ambiance. Such spaces are connected together by a second planning device: a spatial skeleton for the campus body, composed of vistas, axes, lanes, ways, and avenues.

The outstanding example is Central Quad. From that space spring a number of axes that link it both functionally and visually with Liberal Arts Quad to the northeast, with Memorial Way and North Entrance due north, to views of the city and Olympics beyond via Campus Parkway to the west, and—most grandly—along the magnificent Rainier Vista to Science Quad in the southeast, Drumheller Fountain, and of course Mount Rainier beyond. The plan was very much a reflection of the City Beautiful Movement that emerged in American architectural and planning circles at the turn of the century. The great national exhibitions of those years, especially that of Chicago in 1893, did much to stimulate this interest in the beautification of the built environment.

In the years that followed there has on the whole been a remarkable recognition of the unique design circumstances of the campus plan, its architecture, and its landscaping. Despite revisions in later years, the fundamental personality of the campus has been preserved and nurtured. In fact, as of this writing, there is in process a comprehensive examination of the Seattle campus (as opposed to the university's new satellite campuses in Tacoma and Bothell) by a local firm noted for its urban design credentials, which is intended to lead to the creation of a new campus master plan. The firm sought first to discover the campus values shared by the community, encompassing students, faculty, staff, and the people of our neighboring University District:

> A goal of master planning should be to develop buildings and circulation patterns within an open space matrix that is functionally efficient, aesthetically and emotionally rich and supportive and provides inspiration, delight and other intangible qualities to the spirit that either tangibly or intangibly, overtly or covertly, contribute to the quality of the lives of the campus community and in so doing promote the institution's mission of teaching, research and service through providing a setting for this work that is a high quality environment.

Since the 1950s the university has maintained two regulatory design review bodies, the Architectural Commission and the Landscape Advisory Committee. Composed of both local and national design professionals, as well as university representatives, the Commission acts as the client for the university, offering critical review of the architectural designs proposed for construction on campus, with the university holding final

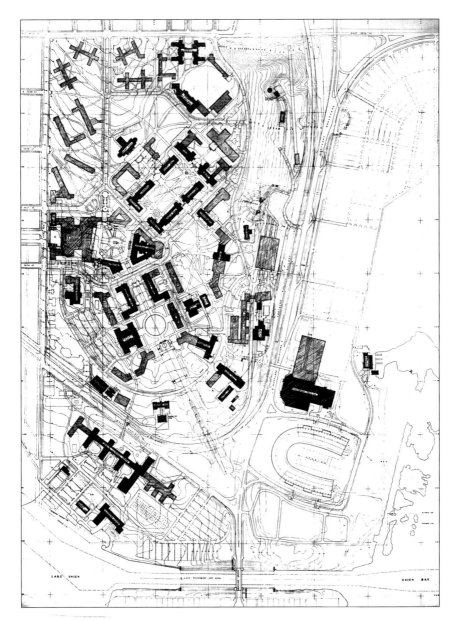

*Campus Plan, 1948*

approval of the project. The Landscape Committee, composed entirely of faculty, staff, and local professionals, holds a similar advisory role affecting site location and landscape aspects of campus projects. By these means, the university exercises its responsibilities for the physical future of the campus. Though there have been some departures from the 1915 Regents Plan, on the whole its objectives and standards have enjoyed a remarkable loyalty in subsequent years of development. In the eleven Walks that lie ahead, the reader will discover to what extent the University of a Thousand Years has been able to protect and enhance the campus vision that the Regents Plan established.

# North-Central Campus

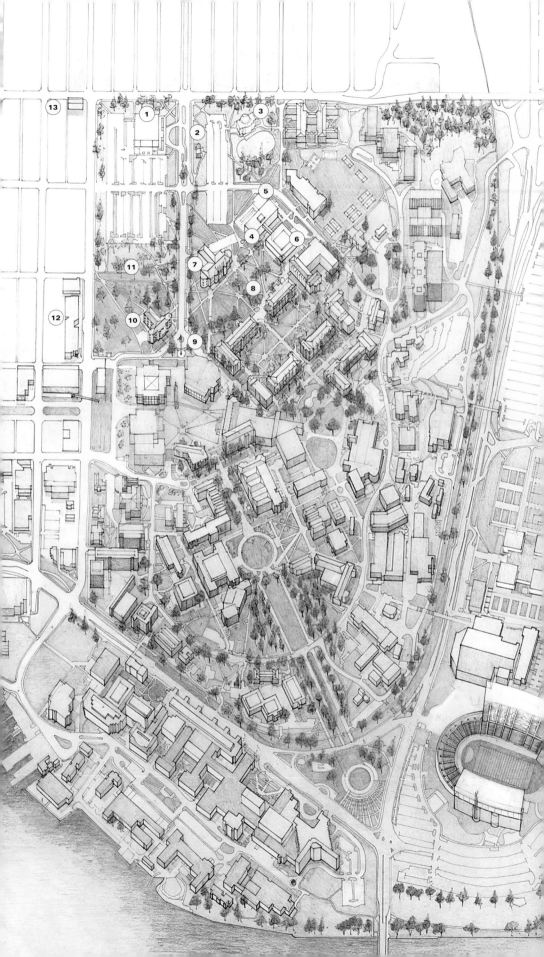

## *Where the University's Roots Are to Be Found*

This is the earliest part of the campus to experience development, containing three of the university's oldest buildings as well as several of the newest ones. In the early days the spaciousness of this area resulted in its use as the university's "front yard," a place for students and faculty to assemble. The more northwesterly corner of the area was wooded until the 1950s, when the parking lots you find there now were built. There are important developments on the horizon likely to impose on its present condition. Proceed from Northeast 45th Street through the 1928 Memorial Gateway pylons. This is Memorial Way, lined with sycamore trees *(platanus x hybrida)* and dedicated to the university students lost in World War I—fifty-seven men and one woman—whose names are found on the bronze plaques of the Gateway pylons.

### 1. Burke Memorial Washington State Museum

*James J. Chiarelli, 1962*

Founded in 1885 by a group of students calling themselves the Young Naturalists Society, the museum was originally housed in a building on the downtown campus, thus making it the oldest university museum in the West. Later the museum occupied the former Washington State Pavilion from the 1909 Alaska-Yukon-Pacific Exposition (AYPE), but its eventual state of dilapidation inspired the construction of the present building. It was erected as a memorial for Judge Thomas Burke, one of Seattle's pioneer leaders, and a bequest for its construction came from his widow, Caroline McGilvra Burke. Involved in display, research, and teaching, the museum is focused mostly directed toward the Pacific Rim cultural and natural heritage. It houses Northwest Coast Native art, various Pacific Coast ethnic group collections, displays of minerals and gems, and the only Northwest dinosaur skeleton.

Initial construction featured what was in effect a kind of structural doughnut, visitors arriving on the upper level surrounding a space open to ground level below. The resulting dramatic height was used to feature freestanding Northwest Indian totem poles. Later to gain further display area the open space was floored over and the poles removed to the landscaped grounds just off the museum's entry drive. Also outside is a wood-carved killer whale at the building's entrance, carved by Professor Emeritus Bill Holm of the School of Art; its form has become the logo of the museum. You will also find near the entrance the recently installed seven-foot bronze Pluma, the work of noted Seattle sculptor Mark Calderon.

*Burke Museum*

Leaving the Museum, consider for a moment the wooded space just due east across Memorial Way but closer to 45th Street. In the early days of the university on its new campus this was the location of what had at one time been a timber-frame water tower, later becoming Chimes Tower. Its fifteen-thousand-pound set of chimes, a donation of Frank Blethen, *The Seattle Times* publisher, was for years played daily by blind pianist George Bailey, class of 1917. The destruction of the tower and chimes in 1949, probably by an arsonist, silenced that tradition for a period. Today, however, the chimes are again heard, played by school of music students who recently re-instituted the tradition.

## 2.   The Observatory    *Charles W. Saunders, 1895*

This building was paid for using both funds and stone that were left over from the construction of the university's first new campus building, Denny Hall. Proclaimed at the time as "the equal of any on the Pacific Coast," its six-inch telescope is sheltered by a dome that rotates on old Civil War cannonballs. Astronomically it is now largely succeeded by far more

*Observatory*

sophisticated remote and computerized televiewing, but there is still an interest in the observatory's free public viewing on selected clear nights. It also offers popular slide show presentations.

*Glen Hughes Penthouse Theater*

## 3. Glenn Hughes Penthouse Theater

*John Ashby Conway and Glenn Hughes, designers; Carl F. Gould, architect, 1940;*
*Boyle/Wagner, Architects, renovation, 1992*

An innovative theater-in-the-round School of Drama program initiated by Glenn A. Hughes, which began in the Penthouse of the University District's Edmond Meany Hotel in 1931, inspired this structure. When in due course it had its new building, located originally on the site of the present Physics/Astronomy complex on lower campus, the school retained the penthouse name for its new ground-level quarters. For its time, the building responded creatively to a fresh approach in theatrical experimentation, the first of its kind in the country. The designers' use of "glue-lam" roof beams expressed the uniqueness of its function—although this technology was little admired at a time when the Collegiate Gothic style was still rigorously adhered to on the campus. In 1992 the building was moved up Fifteenth Avenue with much public acclaim to its present site, undergoing considerable remodeling for its reopening. Its south terrace now faces a fenced open green, which in earlier times served as the women's archery court.

## 4. & 5.  Balmer Hall and SeaFirst Executive Education Center

**Balmer Hall**  *Decker & Christensen and Paul Hayden Kirk, 1962*
**SEEC**  *Kallmann McKinnel and Wood, 1997*

*Balmer Hall*

Though appearing as separate buildings, these are two in one, both representing different design approaches and separated in time and approach but serving the same master, the School of Business Administration. The older of the two, Balmer Hall, was built at a time when the regents had rejected the design constraint of the Collegiate Gothic style, opining that in the mid-twentieth century and with a school of architecture on campus it was time for the university to respond to the ferment of modern design. The early results of this philosophical reorientation are to be seen in Balmer Hall (as well as in its partner to the

*Seafirst Executive Center and Foster Library*

South, Mackenzie Hall; the two were planned simultaneously but built separately). Neither Balmer nor Mackenzie Hall has mellowed much with the years, and more recent ideas to camouflage or even destroy them have not seemed outlandish. Thus the building of a semi-independent SEEC was seen as at least an opportunity to blur Balmer's rather awkward presence. Balmer Hall was named for the late Thomas Balmer, civic leader and university regent.

The SeaFirst Executive Education Center addition and tower are architecturally much more ambitious. The addition includes the Foster Business Library, which offers a handsome new skylit study space. The tower, sited at the curve of Stevens Way, is positioned in partnership with the Collegiate Gothic tower of Hutchinson Hall, the two acting as outposts announcing to the motorists or pedestrians their entry into or exit from central campus. The SEEC tower's design details respond to the Collegiate Gothic stylistic environment, reflecting the Architectural Commission's interest in contextualism. Thus, the tower's brick, cast stone, roof forms, trim, and structural rhythms communicate with its neighbor across the way; the two towers are talking to each other, employing a similar design vocabulary but each with its own distinctive message. With its tower of lofty administrative and teaching spaces, SEEC besides the Library also includes an auditorium, classrooms, student gathering places, and facilities in support of its executive education program.

**6.   Mackenzie Hall**   *Decker & Christensen and Paul Hayden Kirk, 1960*

Mackenzie Hall was named for the former chair of its Department of Accounting, Donald H. Mackenzie, who taught at the university for twenty-two years. Also serving the School of Business Administration, this building houses primarily the School's faculty offices. Its design is another expression of the new design freedom enjoyed by architects on campus in

*Mackenzie Hall*

the second half of the twentieth century, but its aging has not been graceful. There is a pleasant inner court where the bronze Fountain of Reflection is found, a gift to the university by Phi Mu sorority and designed by George Tsutakawa. Tsutakawa, noted for his many successful fountains both in this country and abroad, was for many years a member of the School of Art faculty. This fountain was originally featured in the grounds of the 1962 Seattle World's Fair.

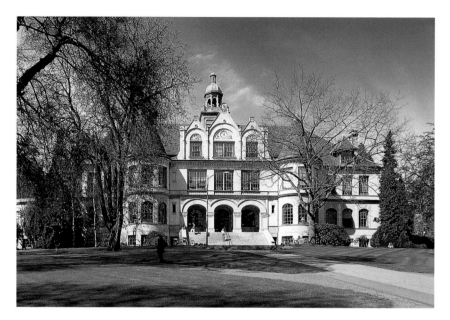

*Denny Hall*

**7. Denny Hall** *Charles W. Saunders, 1895*

Denny Hall is the University of Washington's "Old Main." In contrast to the many red brick versions of these first campus buildings scattered about the country, Denny Hall is a handsome sandstone rendition in the French Renaissance style. Recalling the sixteenth-century chateaux of France, it has aged well in its over one hundred years of service to the university. Originally known as the Administration Building and renamed by the regents in 1910 to honor pioneer Arthur A. and Mary Denny and their family, it was designed to house all the principal university academic and administrative functions, including classrooms, offices, laboratories, a 736-seat auditorium, and the library. Today its versatility is much reduced; it serves primarily the departments of Germanics, anthropology, classics, and near eastern languages and civilization, and the Language Learning Center. Threatened with demolition in the 1950s, it was saved from that fate only to be rather brutally retrofitted internally, so that none of the character of its early interior remains.

As the university's first building on the new campus, Denny Hall continues to play a sentimental role in our history. Its cupola (Gottlieb Weibell crafted it) holds the Varsity Bell, shipped from Troy, New York, "round the Horn" in 1862. Once used to announce classes, it began its university service in the old downtown building where among other occasions it sounded the alarm at the time of Seattle's great fire of 1889. Today it is heard only on Homecoming, with Brewster Denny, '45, Arthur and Mary

Denny's great-grandson, performing the honors. Today the cupola contin-ues to emit bell sounds but via an electronic digital carillon, a pallid substi-tute for those of the Chimes Tower lost by fire in 1949.

## 8. Denny Yard

Denny Yard is roughly defined by Mackenzie Hall to the east, Raitt and Savery to the south, and an open-ended space to the west. It slopes gently down from Denny Hall to provide what was in the early days of the univer-sity a kind of front yard, where special events like campus cleanup day, class picnics, and group photographs occurred. Today it is dominated by a scattering of mature trees, both deciduous and evergreen. Note in particular the monkey puzzle tree (*Araucaria araucana*) with its distinctive silhouette of scaly dark green branches, and nearby a handsome native from the eastern United States, a black walnut (*Jugllans nigra*). Edmond Meany, to convince the legislature to purchase the full acreage of the Interlaken site, had argued that it could also be developed as an arboretum. Though that development never took place, at least on this site, perhaps some of the regularity of tree plantings in Denny Yard and the nearby Campus Green can be credited to that vision.

*Denny Yard*

*World War II Memorial*

### 9.  World War II Memorial  *Jon Gierlich, sculptor, 1999*

The ninety-foot high university Flag Pole near Parrington Hall, on axis with
Memorial Way and Central Plaza, was chosen as the site for Interrupted
Journey, the World War II Memorial, slow in coming to the campus but
finally in place the latter part of 1999. The work of the sculptor Jon Gierlich,
it relies on a simplicity of textured planes, patterns, and roughly hewn stone
pieces carefully placed as intermittent edging to the ensemble. It was conceived as a symbolic journey from order to chaos and back to order, and
was commissioned by the UW Alumni classes of 1943, '44, '45, and '46.

### 10. Parrington Hall
*Josenhans & Allan, 1902; Cardwell Thomas, renovation, 1989*

Located well west of Denny is Parrington Hall, which has provided one of
the pleasantest surprises on the campus in recent years. The building had
been painted early on in an effort to protect its rather porous brick from
moisture seepage; its recent cleaning has revealed an exterior of warm red
brick and sandstone trim. Originally the Science Building, it was remodeled
for use of the English Department. Today it houses the Daniel J. Evans
School of Public Affairs and the Center for Instructional Development and
Research. Its name honors Vernon L. Parrington, who was for twenty-one
years on the English faculty and won the Pulitzer Prize in 1928 with his *Main*

*Parrington Hall*

*Currents in American Thought.* He was quoted as saying the building was "the ugliest I have ever seen." I like to think he would have a different opinion seeing the building today.

Of somewhat uncertain design lineage, it should probably be accepted as Romanesque, austerely interpreted. Originally there was a substantial one-story arched and parapeted front porch, which has been removed. The recent remodeling was done with considerably more sensitivity than that at Denny Hall. The effort to respect the building's historical character reflects current university policy towards rehabilitation.

## 1I. Campus Green

Due north of Parrington Hall is an extensive open lawn, with trees whose planting pattern suggests they might have been placed there as part of Meany's so-called arboretum. It has remained an open space, despite the fact that there were probably intentions to build on it at one time or another. Now much revered, it has been secured as an open green in perpetuity. During the turbulent early 1970s protestors of various stripes, giving it the transitional title of "Hippie Hill," informally occupied it. Now returned to its former serenity and respectability, it was recently again drawn into

*Campus Green*

controversy over the siting of the new Law School Building on its northern perimeter. The new building, which will occupy primarily the existing parking lot to the north, will be designed to enhance rather than blight the green.

### 12. Social Work/Speech and Hearing Sciences Building

*Bebb and Gould (Eagleson Hall), 1922; John Morse, c. 1982; Carlson Architects, renovation, 1999*

*Social Work/Speech and Hearing Sciences Buiding*

This building, cut off by the traffic flows of Fifteenth Avenue Northeast, is something of a campus orphan. A recent third floor remodeling has lightened considerably its rather stolid original design. There is a branch library to serve its disciplines. The Collegiate Gothic Eagleson Hall, completed in 1922, at the building's north end was originally the campus YMCA until acquired by the university, remodeled, and incorporated into and the Social Work/Speech and Hearing Sciences complex.

*Alumni House*

### 13. Alumni House   *Roland Terry, 1963*

Known formally as the R. Bronsdon "Curly" Harris Alumni House, the building—with its rather elegant and sophisticated demeanor—gives little hint of its original role as the Baptist Student Center. Acquired by the University Alumni Association in 1973, it handsomely serves the activities of the association while also memorializing its namesake Curly Harris for his years of service and devotion as the association's executive director from 1936 to 1964.

# East-Central Campus

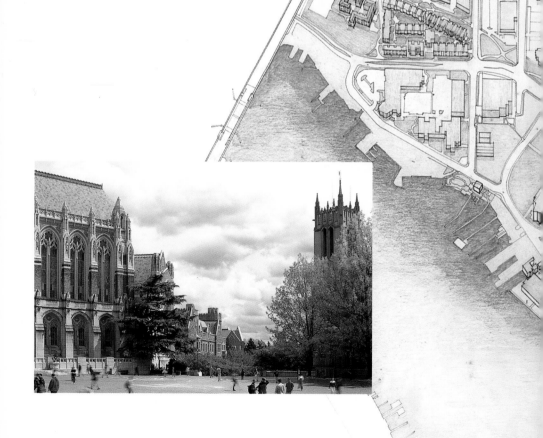

## *Liberal Arts Quad and HUB Yard:*
## *Where the 1915 Regents Plan Begins*

Carl Gould's work on the Regents Plan resolved the design problem of linking the Alaska-Yukon-Pacific Exposition (AYPE) plan of 1909 with that for the original upper campus, which had lain beyond the fair's perimeter. He surmounted that challenge by honoring the confluence of the two principal axes—the southeast-northwest Rainier Vista, which was that of the fair, and a new axis based on the southwest-northeast orientation of the Oval Plan, retained by the Olmsteds in their now abandoned 1906 campus plan. Those axes came together in what became Central Quad, to be visited later. Gould in the Regents Plan gave the Liberal Arts Quad much more compact dimensions, first steps toward its earning a favored status among campus features. It is on this walk that the impact of Collegiate Gothic as the approved architectural style for upper campus first appears. You will also find one of the newest open spaces on campus—HUB yard, with its associated buildings and landscape.

### 14. Liberal Arts Quad

Unlike the upper campus plans of 1898 and 1904, Gould in the 1915 Regents Plan visualized the Liberal Arts Quadrangle as a compact union of space and architecture. Today this quad is a campus favorite: its broad spread of lawns, its bricked walks, the unity of its Collegiate Gothic frame. Especially beloved are its yoshino cherry trees (*Prunus x yedoensis*), transplanted

*Liberal Arts Quad*

there in 1964 when their original location in the University Arboretum—south of the Lake Washington Ship Canal—was obliterated by a freeway connection. In early spring their drifts of pale pink blossoms, the university's own cherry blossom festival, are a seasonal splendor appreciated by all.

### 15. Raitt Hall   *Bebb and Gould, 1916*

*Raitt Hall*

Once the Regents Plan was accepted, the university moved aggressively into a major period of construction. Raitt Hall, the first result of that campaign, was also the university's first exercise in the Collegiate Gothic. Named for Effie Isobel Raitt, director of the then School of Home Economics (a discipline in recent years dropped from the university curriculum), the building gained its priority in the construction schedule by the director's initiative. Not above a certain guile in her approach, She invited legislators to a luncheon in the shack [her existing facilities] and, as luck would have it, it was a rainy day. The roof leaked steadily, lunch was soggy, and a few days later the legislature of 1915 appropriated funds for a new structure for home economics.

The building, true to its gothic roots, includes a series of gargoyles designed by Gould, most of which feature women toiling at domestic work (sewing, cooking, wool-carding). However, there is one bearded male among them—perhaps the architect himself—holding what appears to be a plan of the Liberal Arts Quad (though one commentator saw it as laying down the law!). Gould's partner, Charles H. Bebb, was already a well-established architect in Seattle when Gould joined him in partnership in 1914; Bebb was more responsible for the construction and engineering aspects of their practice, while Gould led their design and planning activities. Today Raitt Hall serves a diversity of programs, including anthropology, comparative medicine, Scandinavian studies, nutritional sciences, and speech communication.

### 16. Savery Hall   *Bebb and Gould, 1917 and 1920*

The ell forming the northwest corner of the Quad was the result of two different construction periods: Commerce Hall in 1917 followed by

*Savery Hall*

Philosophy Hall in 1920 to complete the ell. Both were renamed Savery Hall in 1947 to honor William Savery, who was head of the philosophy department from 1902 until his death in 1947. The onset of America's involvement in World War I delayed the construction of Savery Hall until its later date. The gargoyles are the work of Alonzo Victor Lewis, showing miscellaneous activities; one, however, features General Pershing, the memories of the late war obviously still fresh. Today's occupants continue to include the philosophy department joined by economics and sociology.

*Savery Hall, detail*

### 17. Miller Hall  *Bebb and Gould, 1922*

Next in order of development, William Winlock Miller Hall was originally known as Education Hall. The long stylistic reign of Collegiate Gothic on campus was in large part due to Miller, a powerful regent from 1913 to 1957 and chairman of the Buildings and Grounds Committee. The handsome university seal over the building's northeast entrance serves as a reminder that Miller Hall once also housed the president's office. Other

*Miller Hall*

university administrative activities were here, as well as the education and engineering colleges, the latter of which entertained a sometimes competitive relationship with the architecture students housed on the top floor. The College of Education presently occupies the whole building. The sculptor Alonzo Victor Lewis worked here as well, the figures gracing this building including professors, students, men in top hats, a woman playing a harp, Mercury, and an aged Chinese! The brilliant Virginia creeper on Miller Hall is an autumn pleasure.

### 18. Gowen and Smith Halls

**Gowen Hall** *Abraham H. Albertson, 1932*
**Smith Hall** *Bebb and Gould, 1939*

Gowen Hall, the first building on the Quad not designed by Bebb and Gould, nevertheless continued the university's practice of employing Seattle architects. Abraham Albertson conformed to the basic Collegiate Gothic design of the existing quad neighbors. Originally it was named Condon Hall in recognition of John T. Condon, the first dean of the Law School, for which

*Smith Hall*

the building was originally built. This accounts for the sculptured figures featured in its cornice, great lawgivers of the past, Hammurabi, Moses,

Solon, and the like, the work of sculptor John Elliot. The interiors often are graciously wood-paneled, their aura of tradition helping to explain the turmoil the law school experienced after its move to a brutal and austere new building off campus (to be visited on another walk).

Renamed Gowen Hall, it now memorializes the long academic career of Herbert H. Gowen, an Episcopal minister who was Professor of Oriental Studies at the university from 1909 to 1944. A person of enormous versatility—teaching courses in Chinese, Japanese, Indian, and near eastern literature and history, as well as in religion, Hebrew, Arabic, and Sanskrit— he was a legendary campus figure, walking along, his head in a book. He was said to have read one a day and to have done so until his death at the age of 96 in 1960. The departments of political science, and Asian languages and literature, the society and justice program, as well as the East Asia Library are now among Gowen's occupants.

Smith Hall, appended to Gowen in 1939, was the last structure to appear on the quad before World War II. Again the work of Bebb and Gould, this building exhibits a somewhat more austere interpretation of the prevailing design policy than that seen in its earlier Quad partners. The sculpture is the work of Dudley Pratt, a member of the School of Art faculty. The university brochure, *A Campus Walk*, describes his work on Smith Hall:

> At the east end are six sculptures symbolizing basic human needs and emotions: family, love, shelter, food, rest, and laughter. At the southeast corner are figures depicting the primitive concept of weather. And on the northeast corner is a Buddha-like gargoyle signifying the knowledge of the Orient, a book-laden "egghead" representing the intelligent democracy of America, a World War I soldier in a gasmask as the power of Europe, and a bongo drummer representing the magic of Africa. Of unusual interest are the two groups on the north side portraying Seattle's early history and Seattle in 1939, the year the building was constructed. Among the former are Indians, a totem, a fish, and a cougar. In the latter group are sculptural grotesques of a logger, a construction worker, a trucker, and an engineer clutching what appears to be a slide rule.

Originally called Social Science Hall, it was renamed to honor James Allen Smith, a professor of political science from 1897 to 1924, who also spent eleven of those years as dean of the Graduate School—another of the university's grand old men. It is home base for the departments of history and geography. If you go up a few steps of the entrance at the east end of the building you will find on the wall a large terra cotta bas-relief of the Regents Plan on which the Liberal Arts Quad is based.

## 19. & 20. Art and Music Buildings

**Art Building**  *Whitehouse & Price, 1949; Alfred H. Croonquist, east addition, 1969*
**Music Building**  *Whitehouse & Price, 1950*

*Art Building*

At the conclusion of World War II the university resumed its construction, pressured especially by the sharp GI Bill-inspired enrollment increases of the postwar years. These two buildings, both the work of an architectural firm not from Seattle but from Spokane, closed the east end of the Liberal Arts Quad. Conforming to the design dictates of the time, they established harmonious closure of the quad, their façades, turrets and intervening stairs a rather splendid celebration of the eastward axis.

While ascending the steps, note the purple beech (*Fagus sylvatica var. atropunica*) with its crown of dark purple foliage, claimed by some to be the handsomest tree on campus. In the Art Building to the left, which provides the School of Art studios, offices, and library, seek out the Jacob Lawrence Gallery, named for the noted American painter, a recently deceased member of the Art faculty. Ordinarily it features the work of students and faculty of the School. Outside

*Music Building*

and farther eastward the Art Building forms three sides of the Solomon Katz Memorial, a courtyard designed by Susan Black & Associates, landscape architects in 1997, to honor the late professor, dean of the College of Arts and Sciences, and University Provost and Vice President (1909-1989). Perhaps further landscaping will soften its present somewhat brittle personality. The Music Building to the right has its own library as well as various specialized performance facilities.

### 21. Clark Hall    *Josenhans & Allan, 1899*

Following the move to the new campus, the state legislature appropriated $50,000 for two dormitories, Lewis and Clark Halls, named for the explorers: Clark for women, Lewis for men. Both halls are of brick construction with minimal embellishment. Clark Hall served as a dorm until 1936, except for an interlude during World War I when it was loaned to the Navy for use as an officers' hospital. After 1936 it functioned as the original student union building until the present student center, the HUB, was completed in 1952. Since 1952 Clark Hall has hosted the Air Force, Army, and Navy ROTC programs of the university; as such it was a target of student protests during the turbulent '60s and '70s, including a firebombing in 1969. While the exterior retains much of its original character, remodeling of the interior has entirely removed any architectural character that might have originally existed.

Due south of Clark Hall is an American elm (*Almus americana*), historic for its lineage as a scion of the tree in Cambridge, Massachusetts, where in 1775 George Washington assumed the leadership of the Continental Army. It replaced an earlier elm on campus hit by lightning, and in turn provided a replacement for the one in Cambridge, which suffered a similar fate.

*Clark Hall*

*Communications Hall*

## 22. Thomson Hall and Communications Hall

**Thomson Hall**   *Heath, Gove & Bell/Lea, Pearson & Richards, 1948*
**Communications Hall**   *Heath, Gove & Bell/Lea, Pearson & Richards, 1951 and 1955*

Both of these upper-campus buildings contain classrooms and offices.
Thomson Hall is the base for the Henry M. Jackson School of International
Studies, with its twelve undergraduate and eight graduate programs. The
building is named for David Thomson, who, in his long forty-five-year
tenure as professor of Latin at the university, held an unparalleled number
of academic and administrative positions. Communications Hall houses
the school of communications and, on the ground floor, the dean's office of
the College of Arts and Sciences and its undergraduate advising and computing centers. Economics precluded the possibility of bringing any significant level of detail and enrichment to the architecture. Absent are the
gargoyles and other delights that charm the eye when visiting, say, the
enclosure of Liberal Arts Quad. The buildings define Skagit Lane, which is
lined with horse chestnuts (*Aesculus hippocastanum*), noted for their lively
clustered blossoms in the spring and the autumn harvest of shiny brown
seeds. Just beyond at the southeast corner of Smith Hall you will see a
giant sequoia (*sequoiadendron giganteum*) known as the Edmond L. Meany
sequoia, an appropriate reminder of his interest in the new campus' potential as an arboretum. He always referred to the campus as the "University
grounds and arboretum." This sequoia is one of the few trees left on campus remembered as one of "Meany's trees."

*Grieg Garden*

## 23. Grieg Garden

*Hanna/Olin, Ltd. and Robert Shinbo, landscape architects, 1990*

One of the charms of the campus is the surprise of discovering Grieg Garden. Once a parking lot, it is today a quiet, meditative oasis set in one of the busiest centers of the campus. At the time of planning for the Allen Library, the university saw the opportunity to transform this area into a series of spaces with strong identities. Here you find sculptor Finn H. Frolich's bust of the Norwegian composer Edward Grieg. Originally a feature of the AYPE grounds, the Scandinavian Societies of the Northwest and Alaska gave the sculpture to the university in 1917.

In the Garden notice in particular the blue spruce (*Picea pungens*) near the entrance. A large collection of rhododendrons encloses the garden, transforming the area in the spring with their brilliant colors. The Garden melds to the west into International Grove, a rich setting of trees—the gifts of the various consulates in Seattle at the time of the 1932 bicentennial of George Washington's birth.

*HUB Yard*

**24. HUB Yard**   *Hanna/Olin, Ltd., landscape architect, 1990*

The second of the spaces established in conjunction with Allen Library site planning was HUB Yard, so called because of one of the principal buildings it prefaces, Husky Union Building. At the time of the AYPE this open space was the location for the Washington State Building, which was thereafter used as the University Library, and then subsequently as the Washington State Museum. When the museum moved out, the dilapidated building was torn down, leaving only a partial wing as a reminder of earlier days. The space—nearly empty—then bled off in various directions and lacked any sense of definition, a kind of neglected campus spatial stepchild in obvious contrast to the Liberal Arts Quad. The construction of Allen Library offered the university the opportunity to correct the unfocused quality of the area. Working with the HUB building to the east and Sieg Hall to the south, the architects added the wall of the Allen Library addition to the Yard's west, with an arcade that provided an entry to Grant Lane and also connected the addition to Suzzallo Library. Following the redevelopment of Grieg Garden, the reinstallation of walkways, adjustments to the contours of the land, and a series of defining walls and entryways, suddenly no-place became a place. HUB Yard, with its inviting spaciousness, clustered trees, and (on occasion) sunny lawns, has assumed its rightful place as one of the recognized open space treasures of the campus plan.

There are two especially noble trees in the Yard that were carefully preserved and celebrated by its plan. Just east of the Allen Library tower is a grand Atlas cedar (*Cedrus atlantica*), whose sweeping horizontal branches are reminiscent of the gestures of a ballet dancer. And farther along toward Thomson Hall is another glorious beech tree (*Fagus sylvatica var. atropunica*), this one crowned with copper-colored foliage, especially as it moves into its autumn colors.

*The HUB*

## 25. Husky Union Building (the HUB)

*Bebb and Jones, 1949; Jones and Bindon, Tucker & Shields, 1959; Bindon and Wright,*
*1963; Joyce, Copeland, Vaughan & Nordfors, 1977*

The HUB is located on a site originally occupied during the AYPE by the
heavy-timbered Forestry Building. A facility designed to serve the diversity
of contemporary university campus life, the HUB opened in 1952 and has
since experienced a number of expansions and alterations, paid for with
ASUW (student) funds. One can recognize the succession of architectural
design influences, from an initial modernized version of Collegiate Gothic to
the playful 1960s folded roof plates and the 1977 eastward cafeteria expansion along Stevens Way. The building defines the east edge of HUB Yard,
providing a spatial stage set for student gatherings, protests, campaigns, or
simply lazing in the sun. A variety of student services are housed here: student government offices, TV lounges, games, eateries, a branch of the
University Bookstore, a barbershop, and a ballroom.

On the second floor is a lounge whose fireplace wall features a
1949 mural painting by Ernest Norling displaying a full range of university
history, 1861 to 1926. One can pick out such luminaries as Hiram Conibear
whose rowing crews—equipped with the famous Conibear stroke—went on
to national and international victories (including the 1936 Olympics in
Hitler's Berlin); Coach Gil Dobie of football fame; Regent Kellogg, said to

have held the umbrella that marked the site for Denny Hall; and Clara McCarty holding the first collegiate degree granted by the university; as well as images of the old Chimes Tower (destroyed by arson in 1949); a Husky dog, the university's mascot; and the cornerstone-laying ceremony for Denny Hall on the 4th of July, 1894.

**26. Sieg Hall**  *Harmon, Prey & Dietrich, 1960*

Home to the Department of Computer Science and Engineering, Sieg Hall plays a significant role in defining the south edge of HUB Yard. Have a vote on the least admired building on campus though and Sieg Hall is likely to win hands down! Yet shortly after construction it was lauded in a respected architectural journal as a notable example of modernism, supposedly inspired by the spirit of its Collegiate Gothic neighbors. Irony indeed is at work here, for Lee Paul Sieg, the university's president from 1934 to 1946 whom the building honors, was a firm supporter of the university's original upper campus design policy. Nor does the building lend itself easily to a reworking, each of its many vertical supports having a structural role, virtu-ally eliminating any easy facelift. In the foreground of the HUB, just south of its main entrance, is a memorial in granite and bronze of the 1936–39 Lincoln Brigade; its design reflects the revolutionary fervor of that era.

*Sieg Hall*

## 27. Allen Library   *Edward Larrabee Barnes/John M. Y. Lee & Partners, 1991*

Allen Library is the fourth reincarnation of the university's central library, its anchor being Suzzallo Library of 1927 with later additions. The planning dilemma for this most recent phase was the presence of a major cross-campus pedestrian route, Grant Lane, and how to gain the needed expansion space for Suzzallo while at the same time acknowledging prevailing circulation demands. In his competition presentation to the Architectural Commission, Barnes proposed boldly spanning south over Grant Lane, creating a dramatic arcade announcing entry into HUB Yard, and at the same time extending the building southward to form the Yard's west edge. In site planning it proved to be a winner. A generous donation from Paul Allen, a Seattle Microsoft cofounder, assisted in financing the addition, to be named for his father, Kenneth S. Allen, the library's associate director until his death in 1982. It houses the Natural Sciences Library, Special Collections and Preservation, Manuscripts and University Archives, and library administration offices, besides adding some twenty-five miles of shelving space to the library system.

Enter the Allen Library by its arcade entrance to discover *Raven Brings Light to This House of Stories,* the work of a quartet of artists. A flock of crows (ravens) spiral above the main lobby carrying objects symbolizing language or knowledge, referencing a Native American myth. The work was funded by the state's percent for art program, a required part of campus construction budgets these days. Be sure to visit the lobby's nearby brass Denny Hall Clock, built in 1904 by Gottlieb Weibell. Weibell built the

*Allen Library*

Denny cupola and used the same design for this clock, which was given to the university by his widow in 1959. You will also often find current displays in the exhibition area at the head of the stairs just above the lobby information desk.

Allen Library is an exercise in contextualism, though perhaps only modestly successful. Its choice of materials, the vertical rhythm of its abutments and windows, the gabled roofs, simplified pinnacles, brick patterning, and the rose windows all evoke the campus' Collegiate Gothic past. The building is most successful in its siting and definition of the Yard. Coming from the west, one approaches along Grant Lane, the building signaling by its lofty entry your passage through the arcade. Ahead lies the tower at Allen's east end, which angles south announcing a bend in movement and turning you to head into the yard on axis with the HUB's entrance. Similarly, moving west, Allen tower again announces a bend in movement, guiding you past it and into the arcade and Grant Lane ahead. And this is the route you could take to begin the next campus walk, Central Plaza.

## Central Plaza

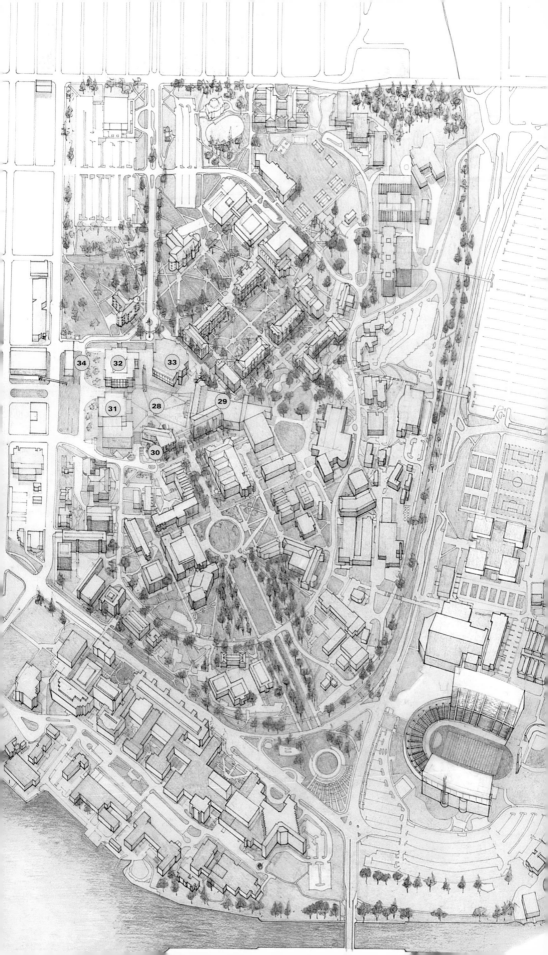

## The Heart of the Campus

Henry Suzzallo, president of the university from 1915 to 1926, envisioned the campus as a union of the arts and the sciences, their physical facilities each clustered separately but joined at some location by certain shared resources—notably, the library, the performing arts spaces, auditoriums, and the administration building. The library, the core symbol of a university, was to be its heart and soul and deserved a location and form commensurate with its intellectual position in the university schema. Understanding this, one can

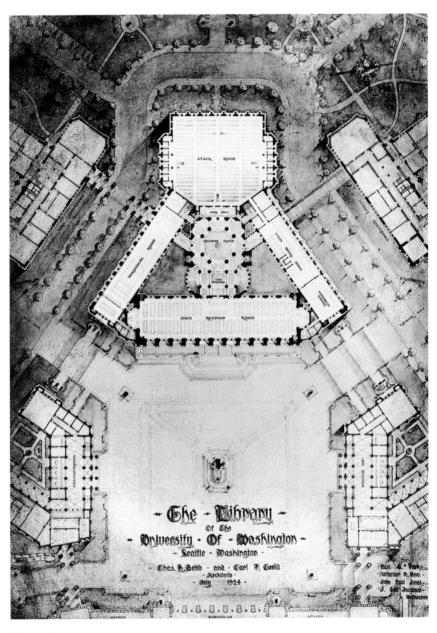

*Library Plan, 1924*

then perceive the philosophical foundation upon which the Regents Plan of 1915 was based and what followed in the way the university was physically planned and built on that foundation.

## 28. Central Plaza

*Kirk, Wallace, McKinley & Associates; Walker and McGough, 1971*

During the Alaska-Yukon-Pacific Exposition of 1909 (AYPE), this was the site of the U.S. Government Building, an enormous pentagonal structure occupying almost the entire space of today's Central Plaza (in common parlance, Red Square). What one sees there today is a relatively recent realization of Suzzallo's dream and the Regents Plan as interpreted in large

*Central Plaza*

part by Carl Gould: a great plaza connecting two major axes, that of the Arts (Liberal Arts Quad) and that of the sciences (Science Quad). These two fields of study are locked together symbolically where their axes meet, at the heart of the university, Central Plaza, the library towering over all of it. It was a powerful vision, remarkably expressed in the campus of the University of Washington. Today's interpretation of that dream is more modest, less symmetrical, and less gothic. It is a generous open space, rather irregularly defined at its perimeter by the forms of the buildings now surrounding it. Its paving is said to be inspired by the great Piazza del Campo in Siena, a brick surface (slippery when wet!) with radiating dividers reaching out from a central low, four-part, concrete slab platform to the plaza's outer edges. Deciduous trees offer some relief, especially when in leaf, from its overall starkness. Dominating the Plaza are three tall clustered brick-clad pylons. Though it is possible to mistake them for an enormous abstract sculpture or the beginnings of a campanile they serve in fact as the vents for the underground garage below the plaza.

At one corner just off the Liberal Arts axis to the northeast is noted painter/sculptor Barnett Newman's two-ton, twenty-six-foot-high steel sculpture, Broken Obelisk. A gift to the university from the Virginia Wright Fund in 1971, the piece is in wonderful harmony with its environment, as if it had been specifically designed for it, but instead is a happy coincidence. As noted in a University Information Center brochure, Newman created the obelisk from fabricated Cor-ten steel that now has weathered to a rusty brown. Its amazing point-counter-point balance has attracted numerous photographers, particularly in the late afternoon when it casts a dramatic shadow across the brick paving.

## 29. Suzzallo Library

*Bebb and Gould, 1926; Bebb and Jones, 1935; Bindon and Wright, 1963*

Suzzallo's vision for the Plaza buildings was slow to be achieved though it had a healthy start with the construction of the first phase of his library (it was named for Suzzallo in 1933). The central location for the library was all that he could have wanted, dominating the Plaza and its axial connections. As visualized by Gould, it was conceived in an ambitious Collegiate Gothic style, its equilateral triangle plan fitting neatly into the conjunction of the two axes. A towering campanile, thrusting above the core of the triangle, was to express the dominant role of the library in the physical and intellectual life of the institution. Planned as a project of sequential construction phases, the library saw the completion of the first phase, the west face of the triangle, in 1926. This was followed in 1935 by the second construction phase, the south face of the triangle. But the third face and the tower were never built. By the time the university was ready for the library's further expansion, architectural design standards had changed, resulting in a 1963 glass and concrete confection that answered the space needs of the time but contributed little to the university's architectural reputation.

The 1926 building is the acme of the university's Collegiate Gothic era, rich in iconography realized in architectural ornament such as friezes, glass, metalwork, cast stone, terra cotta, and brick. Alan Clark, a Tacoma sculptor, executed the series of three figures at the main entrance: the bearded old man, Thought, a woman to his right, Inspiration, and a male figure, Mastery, on his left. Above them on the buttresses across the face of the building are four-and-a-half-feet tall terra-cotta figures representing the major contributors to learning and culture. The faculty selected these figures out of some 246 nominations; from left to right: Moses, Pasteur, Dante, Shakespeare, Plato, Franklin (the only American), Justinian, Newton, da Vinci, Galileo, Goethe, Herodotus, Adam Smith, Homer, Gutenberg,

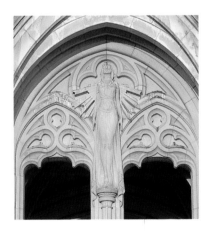

*Suzzallo Library, detail*

*Suzzallo Library, detail*

*Bebb and Gould Library*

Beethoven, Darwin, and Grotius. Note also the gothicized lettering of the academic fields on the belt course just above the first-floor windows, and the shields of other universities between the reading room windows.

Enter the building and ascend the sweeping stairs to the second level, passing by the Jon Geise sculpture, *Circum Okto,* and into the main reading room—one of the finest architectural spaces in the state. Seventeen tall lancet windows line its cathedral-like dimensions, each with their own tales to tell. Each features a medallion of the watermarks used by early printers, as well as other decorative devices; Charles W. Smith, the reference librarian at the time and later university librarian for forty-two years, worked with the architects in developing them. Notice also the oak friezes, carved by H. L. Erickson, above the bookshelves, featuring plant materials native to the state. The architects for the room designed the long oak tables.

It was almost ten years later before the library received its second phase addition, the south wing of 1935. Seamlessly matching the style of the original structure, this wing contains the notable Smith Room, named for the aforementioned librarian. Its splendid iconography, especially its west window and the many medallions, references many regional and historical events.

When the 1960s had their turn with Suzzallo Library, in the third phase addition, there was only the barest reference to the past. By this time the architectural profession had freed itself of stylistic eclecticism in favor of modernism and function. The hint of gothic arches on the exterior of the

*Suzzallo Library*

1963 Suzzallo addition of exposed concrete and glass is at its best tenuous.

And finally there was the 1991 addition, the Allen Library, which is included in Walk Two. The whole ensemble became the Suzzallo-Allen Library, together with the Odegaard Undergraduate Library across Central Plaza.

## 30. Gerberding Hall  *Victor N. Jones and John T. Jacobsen, 1949*

The Administration Building, renamed for William P. Gerberding in 1995 at the time of his retirement after sixteen years as university president, was the first building to be built on the Plaza following World War II. Of cast stone, it is the most pretentious of the buildings in the last years of the Collegiate Gothic style, fully utilizing that vocabulary with towers, pointed arches, pinnacles, sculpted bosses and gargoyles. Along the parapet are to be found a series of sculptures by Dudley Pratt, depicting campus disciplines—note especially that of Father Neptune representing oceanography and fisheries on the east gable end. Liberal Arts are featured on the tower, including Phi Beta Kappa keys as well as a profile of Herbert T. Condon, a "Friend of Youth," the dean of students in the '40s. Bronze seals of the territory and state of Washington as well as the university are found on the

*Gerberding Hall*

plaza face of the building; its use for university administration is recalled by the gowned figure above the entry porch with a money bag in one hand and an adding machine in the other. The building also houses the offices of the dean and the administration of the Graduate School.

Following the construction of Gerberding Hall there was a long hiatus in which the great expanse of space, lawn, and crisscrossing paths before Suzzallo Library lay fallow. Due west of Suzzallo stood the old Meany Hall, the auditorium building—a holdover from the AYPE. Already partially condemned due to safety considerations, it was awkwardly located in terms of long-range planning for this central area. While some decision on its fate was still to be made the forces of nature intervened. A substantial earthquake in 1965 severely damaged the building, resulting in its complete condemnation and removal. Suddenly this central area was eligible for a complete reworking and the achievement of President Suzzallo's vision for a great Central Plaza. There followed in quick succession the underplaza garage and the rest of the buildings defining Central Plaza today.

### 31. Meany Hall

*Kirk, Wallace, McKinley & Associates, 1974; Hewitt Isley, renovation, 1994*

The last of the new buildings surrounding Central Plaza, Meany Hall is a major university and community resource. Its auditoriums serve the performing arts of music and dance, and its main 1200-seat auditorium is a notable acoustical success. The building also has a smaller studio theater, dance studio, offices, lounges, rehearsal rooms and instrument and

*Meany Hall*

costume storage. In the main lobby and in various other locations one finds an intriguing range of art work, including that of Dale Chihuly, George Tsutakawa, Jacob Lawrence, Guy Anderson, and others, representing a rich panoply of Northwest artists, many of whom are teaching or have taught at the university. Meany Hall has had a difficult structural history—its original brick veneer proved to be inadequately anchored to the building's reinforced concrete shell. The resulting replacement of the brick facing in 1994 afforded the opportunity to make changes in some of the exterior features: redesigned main entrances, a series of skylights, and a brick patterning recalling that traditional campus practice.

*Odegaard Undergraduate Library*

### 32. Odegaard Undergraduate Library

*Kirk, Wallace, McKinley and Associates, 1972*

In 1973 at the time of Charles E. Odegaard's retirement from the university presidency, after a notable fifteen-year tenure, this library was renamed in his honor. Sheathed in brick veneer, it has an interesting exterior whose forms, shades, and shadows reflect its internal organization of study carrels. There is a dramatic central space with stairs ascending upward to the successive levels of the building. On the second floor is Everett DuPen's bronze bust of Odegaard, a gift to him from the University Alumni Association and the Board of Regents at the time of his retirement. The third floor contains yet another remembrance, the Odegaard portrait by Ted Rand. The library also houses *By George*, an eatery entered from the lower terrace level to the south.

### 33. Kane Hall *Walker, McGough, Foltz, Lyerla, 1971*

Kane Hall completes the encirclement of Central Plaza, the rather brutal vertical rhythm of its concrete structural bays reminiscent of those on Suzzallo—though without their elegance. Within is a series of auditoriums, the largest of which is the Theodore Roethke Auditorium, honoring the late Pulitzer Prize-winning poet and member of the faculty. Above the second floor lobby is the 1945 Shipscalers Mural, painted by Pablo O'Higgins for the lobby of a Seattle union hall, later put away in storage and forgotten. Rediscovered in 1975, it has found a happy home in Kane Hall. Also on the second floor is a kind of university ceremonial parlor, the Walker Ames

*Kane Hall*

Room, a space of considerable spatial grandeur. It is named for a family whose generous gifts to the university include the President's Mansion in nearby Madison Park. At one end of the Ames Room is the charming carved wood case for the Littlefield Organ, dedicated in 1990.

## 34. Henry Art Gallery

*Bebb and Gould, 1927; Gwathmey Siegel and Associates*
*and Loschky, Marquardt & Nesholm, renovation and addition, 1996*

President Suzzallo's ambitions for the university included an art museum that would be available both to the campus and to the general community. Seattle at that time did not have a public art museum. A private collection did exist, however, owned by Horace C. Henry, whose fortune had come from real estate and railroads. Both President Suzzallo and Carl Gould were part of Henry's social circle, and the President (and no doubt his favorite architect) recognized the potential of the Henry collection as the donated nucleus for a university museum. Suzzallo was successful in

Broken Obelisk

*Henry Art Gallery*

1926 in gaining from Henry not only the collection (appraised at that time at some $300,000 to $500,000) but also a gift of $100,000 for the construction of a gallery to house it. The Henry Art Gallery has over the years and especially more recently built a unique reputation, active in the flourishing art scene of present day Seattle and in a regional and national setting as well.

The site of the original museum building on the west edge of campus had been allocated in the Regents Plan for a huge multi-purpose building to serve the visual and performing arts, accessible equally from campus and community. The Henry (its familiar moniker) was designed as an initial wing of that complex. Architecturally noted for the bold simplicity of its two-story, patterned brick-clad and cast stone-trimmed windowless form, the building is relieved by allegorical figures and designs by Dudley Pratt with ancient Egyptian, Greek, medieval European, and Asiatic references.

The 1927 gallery building never became an adjunct of the proposed arts ensemble. By the 1990s the museum's mission was seriously limited by its modest facilities. Successful fund-raising efforts supported the construction of an extensive addition, recently completed. Now an independent entity, the Henry has splendid new spatial versatility both for its traditional roles and as for its work as an art activist institution. To realize its dreams for a "signature building," The Henry turned to an internationally prominent New York firm, Gwathmey Siegel & Associates. In turn, the university's Architectural Commission bent its standards to allow an innovative departure from the prevailing campus contextualism. The result has borne both plaudits and buffets from its public, but it does demonstrate on the part of university administrators that the review process need not ossify creativity. Whatever its local repute may be, the Henry Art Gallery has the distinction of being the only campus building on which an entire book has been written.

Just inward from The Henry and facing west on axis with Campus Parkway is the university's first major art acquisition, the heroic bronze of George Washington by the nationally noted sculptor Lorado Taft. It is one of a number of sculptures that became permanent campus features with the closing of the AYPE. The local Daughters of the American Revolution, seeing it as an ideal embellishment for the fair and also as an occasion to honor the first president, instigated a $30,000 statewide campaign for its purchase. Although other DAR chapters, individuals, businesses, and school children were asked to join in the funding effort, results were limited. Ultimately, the state legislature made up the deficit with a $20,000 grant to complete payment for both statue and base. For a time Washington stood facing westward on line with the 40th Street entrance to the fair and later the campus, but with completion of Campus Parkway and the more recent Central Plaza improvements he now stands permanently as a monumental reminder of our national history, in the state and the university named for him.

# South-Central Campus and Science Quad

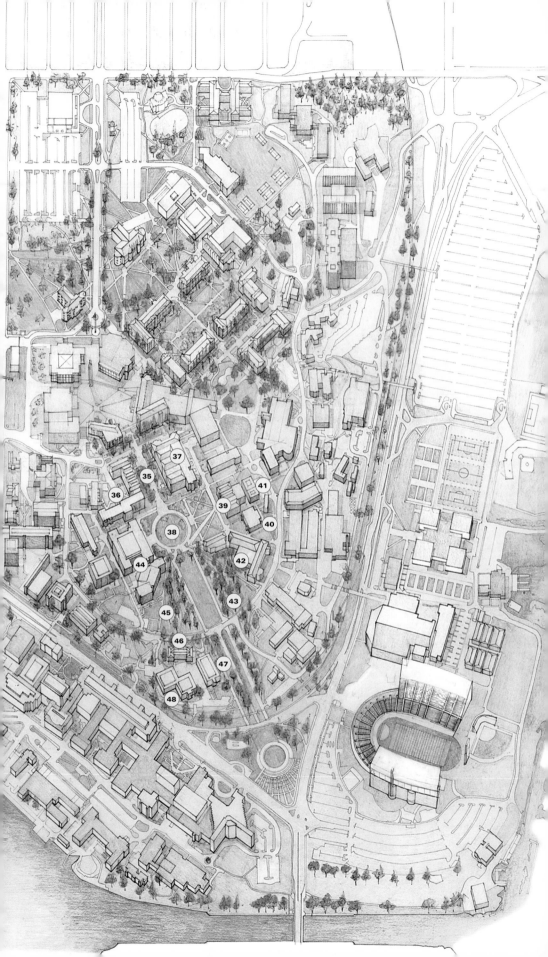

## *Where the Sciences Take Over*

Moving into the lower campus is to follow the Rainier Vista axis out of Central Plaza as it establishes linkage with Science Quad. The view down the Vista on those wonderful occasions when Mount Rainier is out in all its glory is one of the superb bonuses realized by John C. Olmsted when he returned to the campus in 1906 to begin planning for the Alaska-Yukon-Pacific Exposition (AYPE), making the Vista the major visual theme of the grounds.

**35. Rainier Vista**  *Olmsted Brothers, landscape architects, 1906–1909*

Inspired by the view of Mount Rainier, Olmsted made this axis the heart of the AYPE plan. During the fair monumental exhibition buildings evocative of Roman imperial architecture, in the style established by the 1893 Columbian Exposition in Chicago, lined this walkway. The majority of the buildings, being of temporary lath and plaster construction, were torn down after the fair, leaving the axis open for future development. A water cascade and elaborate landscaping dominated the center of the axis during the fair; now entirely gone, they have been replaced by paving. Rainier Vista has been granted a level of sacredness that protects it and inspires architectural

*Rainier Vista*

and landscaping initiatives that further reinforce its drama. The ensemble is a brilliant example of *shakei*, the Japanese garden planning principle of borrowed landscape. Some Hisakura cherry trees (*Prunus serrulata*) at the Vista's north end add their seasonal pleasure to the scene. Farther south, where Stevens Way crosses the Vista, is a bronze plaque memorializing the 1909 AYPE as the inspiration for the Vista and much of the campus plan. Just south of it are two rows of Kwanzan cherry trees (*Prunus serrulata*) paralleling the Vista, the gift of members of the Tokyo alumni group.

## 36. Johnson Hall, Atmospheric Sciences-Geophysics Building, and Quaternary Research Building

**Johnson Hall**   *John Graham, 1930*
**Atmospheric Sciences-Geophysics Building**   *Durham, Anderson & Freed, 1970*
**Quaternary Research Building**   *Durham, Anderson & Freed, 1973*

Johnson Hall and its partner across the Vista to the east, Physics (now Mary Gates) Hall, were conceived as the architectural frame for Rainier Vista after it crosses Grant Lane. Their generous setbacks also provide opportunities for landscaping, enhancing the Vista. Johnson Hall honors the versatile career of Orson B. Johnson, professor of the multiple disciplines of physiology, botany, zoology, biology, mineralogy, geology, chemistry, and natural philosophy! His retirement in 1910 must surely have been well earned. Today the Hall serves primarily the department of geological sciences, which seeks a greater understanding of regional and world earthquakes, and some activities of the

*Atmospheric Sciences–Geophysics Building*

department of botany. Technically, since both it and its partner, Mary Gates Hall, are on lower campus, they need not have adhered to the Collegiate Gothic style. However, the architects and no doubt the regents opted for that design route, so these two buildings reflect the dominant traditional style of the campus.

Attached to Johnson Hall to the west is the Atmospheric Sciences-Geophysics Building and the Quaternary Research Building, the former

*Johnson Hall*

home for the department of atmospheric sciences and the geophysics
program. Quaternary research is a
highly specialized technology that
focuses on the processes that have
shaped the natural environment in
roughly the last two million years;
some of the research requires underground facilities.

### 37. Mary Gates Hall (formerly Physics Hall)

**Physics Hall**   *John Graham, 1928*
**Mary Gates Hall**   *Hartman-Cox with Bassetti Architects, 2000*

Johnson Hall's sibling, Mary Gates Hall, has undergone a complete renovation of both form and purpose. With the physics department having recently
moved to its new quarters on campus, Physics Hall no longer served the
sciences. Dedicated in May 2000 by Microsoft chairman Bill Gates in honor
of his mother, the building is now home to the Dean of Undergraduate
Education, an Undergraduate Computing Center, the university's new
Information School, and classrooms—a reflection of the attention the university is giving to its undergraduate students and programs. What was
originally an ell-shaped building has become a rectangular doughnut with a

*Mary Gates Hall*

glamorous skylit central "commons," around which the various activities of the center cluster. Viewed externally, the building's design makes a seamless connection between the old Physics Hall fabric and the new addition. The observer might well wonder what happened to the modern movement in architecture and the events that revolutionized the profession over the last one hundred years, when nothing hints of it between this 1928 building and its 2000 wing.

## 38. Science Quadrangle and Drumheller Fountain
*The AYPE and Regents Plans*

The buildings that today give form the Science Quad represent a phased development, beginning with Johnson and Mary Gates Halls and closing with the very recent construction of the Bagley addition and the expansion of the Computer Sciences & Engineering Building. The design of the area had its roots in the AYPE's Geyser Basin, a circular pool with a modest central jet encircled by temporary fair display buildings. The Quad was featured in the 1915 Regents Plan and later further elaborated by Bebb and Gould. The pond is commonly known as Frosh Pond on account of an early tradition of tossing freshmen into it, a practice now less observed. You are more likely to see ducks and Canadian Geese in it today.

The quadrangle's principal feature is Drumheller Fountain by Lawrence Halprin, with its 100-foot central jet, the gift of former regent Joseph Drumheller of Spokane on the occasion of the university's

*Science Quadrangle and Drumheller Fountain*

centennial observances in 1961. Unlike Liberal Arts Quad, Science Quad never had a very complete sense of enclosure, especially to the southeast, which should be a gateway through which Rainier Vista continues onward toward distant Mount Rainier. As will be explained shortly, more recent construction has managed to enhance and underscore that gateway and the view beyond. Just to the south of the fountain and on the axis of Rainier Vista is the Class of 1912 Sundial of rough-hewn granite and bronze. When the World War II Memorial was recently installed, the sundial was moved to this new location.

### 39. Guggenheim Hall   *John Graham, 1929*

Guggenheim Hall is another example of a lower campus building following in the Collegiate Gothic stylistic tradition, despite its location outside that campus policy's dictates. The Daniel Guggenheim Fund donated the money for its construction, to encourage aeronautical engineering and to "assist in making air transportation safe, popular, and regularly available." Guggenheim himself never saw the results of his fund's generosity, as he died in the year following its completion. Architecturally, the building is a handsome interpretation of its genre; especially notable is the lovely main entrance with its cast stone gothic traceries and wood-paneled entrance doors. The Hall's primary occupant is the department of aeronautics and astronautics.

*Guggenheim Hall*

*Guggenheim Hall, detail*

*Aerospace and Engineering Research Building*

## 40. Aerospace and Engineering Research Building

*Young, Richardson and Carleton, 1969*

In sharp contrast architecturally with its Guggenheim neighbor to the north, this building represents a phase of 1960s design found elsewhere on campus in a few examples. It is boldly expressed as a brick cube with deep-set windows enclosing four floors of test chambers, faculty offices, and areas for gas mechanics, wave propagation, and antenna research. Here of course one finds the aerospace and engineering research program.

## 41. Kirsten Wind Tunnel and Aerodynamics Laboratory

**Kirsten Wind Tunnel**   *Bebb and Gould, 1937*
**Aerodynamics Laboratory**   *1917*

Originally known simply as the Wind Tunnel, the Kirsten Wind Tunnel as it is now called honors Frederick K. Kirsten, a member of the faculty from 1915 to 1952 and the holder of over one hundred patents. Some may remember his briefly popular Kirsten pipe, which he invented before World War II; its specially designed metal

*Kirsten Wind Tunnel*

stem was to permit cooler smoking. The tunnel provides testing for aircraft and other structures at high wind speeds. It tested models for a new Narrows Bridge in Tacoma, after the infamous first bridge failed in 1940 when undergoing severe wind conditions. It has since been used to test such structures as the Seattle Space Needle, Husky Stadium, and nearly all of Boeing's commercial airplanes.

To the southeast of Kirsten Lab one finds the precursor of the Kirsten Tunnel, the little wood-frame and rather elegant Aerodynamics Laboratory, a 1917 gift to the university by William Boeing. At that time there were only two other such wind tunnel installations in the country, one at M.I.T. (whose tunnel specifications ours would match), the other at the Navy Yard in Washington, D.C. Its construction marked the beginning of the university's aeronautics program and served the nascent Boeing Aeroplane Company, helping it to become a major player in the developing airplane industry. The installation of a new open circuit subsonic wind tunnel has enabled it to continue its useful life on the campus.

### 42. Computer Sciences and Engineering Building

*Paul Thiry, 1948; addition, 1972; Kallmann McKinnell & Wood and Mahlum & Nordfors, addition, 1999*

The original building for computer sciences and engineering was the work of one of Seattle's major architects, Paul Thiry. A University of Washington graduate, he went on to a career of national and international

*Computer Sciences and Engineering Building*

*Computer Sciences and Engineering Building*

dimensions. The original wing facing Stevens Way forms his major architectural project on campus, though he also played an important role in some of the campus planning discussions and decisions in the evolutionary years following World War II. Strictly a modernist in architectural design, Thiry was a central force in introducing more recent design trends to the Seattle scene, entirely rejecting any Collegiate Gothic gestures in his work. This building honors his beliefs and approach. Note the three sculptured panels, the work of Everett DuPen. Thiry had requested that they be expressive of the power of electricity; DuPen, however, chose to go in more conventional directions. In 1972 a fourth floor was added to the building.

The current westward expansion enormously increases the size of the building, and also strengthens the spatial definition of Science Quad. Prior to the building's development, the southeast face of the Quad was only weakly established, primarily by the trees of both the Sylvan Theater to the east of Rainier Vista and Island Grove to the west as the gateway through which Rainier Vista extended onward toward the mountain. The Computer Sciences and Engineering Building to the left (with the Chemistry Building addition to the right) provided the opportunity to add architectural enclosure to dramatize both the perimeter of Science Quad and the gateway through which Rainier Vista passes. Architecturally, the building is an important example of contextualism. Its forms, materials, and details suggest an affinity with its neighbors but are interpreted in ways clearly marching to its own drummer. Its plan also coordinates with Sylvan Theater's landscaping to preserve that area's sanctuary. (A second expansion phase for computer sciences and engineering is being planned which will require demolition of the 1948 structure. )

In the building's entrance is Winsor Ceiling, a rotunda ceiling sculpture by Jackie Winsor that suggests the night sky, paying homage to historic domed ceilings while in reality being very nearly flat. Room 3 has a nationally noted permanent art exhibit composed in part of forty-four tiles mounted on desk fronts, a design by Louise St. Pierre and Karen Cheng. On the second floor there is an attractive three-story skylit study atrium that features an art display drawn from the School of Art student collection. The building is home to the computer sciences and engineering department's offices, classrooms, and laboratories, Planned construction would accommodate future program requirements.

## 43. Sylvan Theater

The campus retains a few places in a natural state, reminding one of its early wooded days and offering quiet retreats from the active bustle of most of the campus. Sylvan Theater is one of those places. During AYPE days the Theater was the location for the Music Pavilion, a Greek temple surrounded by a protective belt of landscaping. The temple is long gone but some of the trees remain, augmented by later additions. The Theater's space is domi-

*Sylvan Theater*

nated at one end by four Ionic columns—they and the Denny Bell atop Denny Hall are the only remnants of the university's original downtown campus to find a place on the new one. When the old Territorial Building was destroyed in 1911 the columns were moved to the new campus, first just south of Denny Hall but in 1924 to the Theater. Edmond Meany had sought to preserve the whole Territorial Building but had to settle for this front entrance colonnade. It was Herbert T. Condon who gave them the acronym, L.I.F.E.: Loyalty, Industry, Faith, and Efficiency. Seek out in the plantings to the west a memorial dedicated to General Lafayette of Revolutionary War fame, a gift of the state's French residents in 1934, a century after his death. In earlier days an occasional setting for graduations, or for pre-World War II Songfests, these days the enclosure is mostly silent, a place for quiet talks, a memory-filled walk, an al fresco picnic.

## 44. Bagley Hall and the Chemistry Building

**Bagley Hall**  *Naramore, Granger & Thomas with Carl Gould, 1937*
**Chemistry Building**  *Moore, Ruble, Yudell with Loschky, Marquardt & Nesholm, 1995*

Daniel Bagley, who contributed significantly to securing the university's Seattle location and its early history, is appropriately remembered in the naming of this building. His name had earlier been given to the AYPE's Fine Arts Building, one of the fair's permanent buildings, afterwards used by the

*Bagley Hall and the Chemistry Building*

university as its chemistry building. When that department moved into this 1937 building it brought the Bagley name with it. At the time of construction it was the university's most expensive project to date, costing some $l.2 million, big money for those days. The classrooms, labs, and offices of the department of chemistry are housed here. In a way its design represents early contextualism, a modernized "art deco" interpretation of Collegiate Gothic that has worn well over the years. Note in the entrance lobby two large 1936 mosaic murals by Robert B. Inverarity. A WPA Federal Art Project, they depict the contributions of Egyptian alchemy and modern science to chemistry.

The 1995 addition to Bagley, the Chemistry Building provides offices, classrooms, and labs that augment those in Bagley Hall. Its four large stacks are the combined exhaust vents for the entire building. In addition, it was specifically sited to accomplish several objectives. Like the Computer Sciences and Engineering Building to the east, it emphasizes the southeast enclosure of Science Quad and serves as a gateway for the extension of Rainier Vista. But the Chemistry addition was also sited parallel to the diagonal of Garfield Lane to maintain the axis up the lane from Stevens Way to Drumheller Fountain's central jet. Thus, Science Quad has become a key university exercise in the art of urban design.

## 45. Medicinal Herb Garden, Island Grove, and Hellmuth/Reynolds Bus Shelters

Due south from Chemistry Building is the university's Medicinal Herb Garden, reconfigured when this area was reworked to accommodate the new building and Garfield Lane. The garden had its beginnings in 1911, at a time when the Department of Pharmacy was far more dependent on drugs provided by nature rather than those from Pharmacy's test tubes. The latter trend orphaned the garden, in spite of its long history of service, but in recent years it has been adopted by the volunteer group Friends of the Medicinal Herb Garden, which has undertaken the garden's care. Its geometric beds, plants, and explanatory labels, which spread both west and east of the Garfield Lane axis, offer interesting displays for the visitor. The garden's original entrance at its western end is marked by monkeys atop two flanking columns, evocative of Italian medieval medicinal herb gardens, for which monkeys were a traditional symbol.

Island Grove to the east of Garfield Lane is bisected from north to south by Island Lane. Walking its length gives perhaps the best glimpse of what the university campus must have been like in its predevelopment days. At its south end is an open space, the easterly portion of the Herb

*Medicinal Herb Garden, Island Grove, and bus shelter*

Garden. It is bordered by some mature trees, which include a large cucumber tree (*Magnolia acuminata*), whose crimson seeds are borne in bright red conelike pods, a native of the eastern U.S.; a handsome Pacific dogwood (*Cornus nuttallii*), a great Puget Sound favorite; and a northern catalpa tree (*Catalpa speciosa*), another Eastern and Middle Eastern native. Just to the west of Island Lane at its end is another grand Sierra redwood (*Sequoiadendron giganteum*).

Returning to Garfield Lane, to the west you will find on both sides of Stevens Way two wood-frame bus shelters, the work of visual artists Suzanne Hellmuth and Jock Reynolds, another project supported by the state's percent for art program. In the more southerly station are a display area and brochures for self-guiding on the C. Frank Brockman Memorial Tree Tour, which will lead you on a full-campus tour and viewing of all the major trees. In this area, also westward and along Stevens Way, begin magnificent parallel rows of deodar cedars (*Cedrus Deodara*). Their upright cones (candles) in the fall sprinkle the ground and Stevens Way with bright yellow-green pollen.

**46. Anderson Hall**  *Bebb and Gould, 1925*

*Anderson Hall*

Anderson Hall across Stevens Way from Island Grove is one of lower campus's more elaborate exercises in the Collegiate Gothic style. It also has the distinction of being the first building the university received as a gift, when in the early 1920s Agnes H. Anderson gave the funds for it in memory of her lumberman husband, Alfred Anderson. Its Stevens Way facade, symmetrically organized around the entrance porch, is framed at either end by tall gabled roofs above traceried pointed-arch windows. At its easterly end is another redwood, this one a coast redwood (*Sequoia sempervirens*). Anderson Hall is home to the College of Forest Resources.

**47. Winkenwerder Forest Sciences Laboratory**

*Grant, Copeland, Chervenak & Associates, 1963*

In the design for Winkenwerder Lab, located just east of Anderson Hall, a conscious effort was made to demonstrate the structural versatility and visual elegance of timber. A system of columns and beams creates the skeleton for glass-enclosed laboratories. It was named for Hugo Winkenwerder, the College of Forest Resources dean from 1912 to 1945.

*Winkenwerder Laboratory*

**48. Bloedel Hall**   *Grant, Copeland, Chervenak & Associates, 1971*

This is second of the two buildings augmenting Anderson Hall with forest resources teaching and research support. It also demonstrates the potentials that wood offers for finish and structural applications. Bloedel Hall, located behind Anderson Hall, also houses the college's library. The exterior courtyard formed by these three Forestry buildings has been designed for conversation, lunches, and circulation. It was originally designed by Richard Haag (a retired UW landscape faculty member) and later modified by William Talley, landscape architect. Bloedel Hall honors Julius H. Bloedel, another pioneer lumberman who built a reputation of generosity with the college through his support for scholarships and research.

*Bloedel Hall*

# Southwest Central Campus

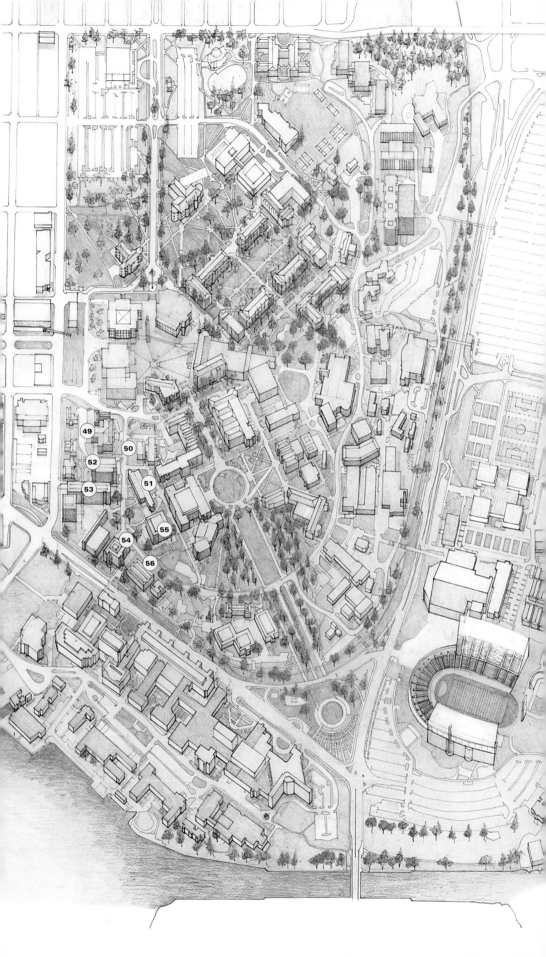

## *Where the University's AYPE Architectural Remnants Remain*

When the university made its deal with the sponsors of the 1909 Alaska-Yukon-Pacific Exposition (AYPE) and loaned the undeveloped southern section of the campus to them, the sponsors in turn agreed that certain buildings should be constructed of a permanent nature and be turned over afterwards for university purposes. Most construction for the fair, however, was temporary, to be torn down or in a few cases left to the university for whatever useful life they might retain. On this walk two AYPE buildings, one permanent and one temporary, are to be found.

### 49. Architecture Hall

*Howard & Galloway, 1909; Boyle-Wagner Architects, renovation, 1987*

Just south of the university's Fortieth Street entrance and guard gate is Architecture Hall, one of the half dozen or so permanent buildings erected for the fair. The Fine Arts Building was designed by the supervising AYPE architect, John Galen Howard of California. Its style is modestly classical in cream colored brick and terra cotta. At the time of the fair it had a larger design sibling farther north on campus, the fair's auditorium building. That building, subsequently known as Meany Hall, remained in use until extensively damaged in the region's 1965 earthquake. Thus, Architecture Hall stands alone as a reminder of the monumentality of the 1909 fair.

Once the university assumed ownership, the building was equipped for use as the Chemistry Building and renamed Bagley Hall to honor that early and influential university sponsor. On completion of the 1937 Bagley Hall, Chemistry moved into it, freeing the former AYPE building for the physiology and the architecture programs. The architecture program expanded to such a degree that in 1957, with the creation of the College of Architecture and Urban Planning, the building was renamed Architecture Hall to acknowledge its principal tenant.

On the third floor will be found a student-operated coffee shop, which had a rather revolutionary role in the early 1960s. The architecture students had decided that a coffee shop in the building would not only serve their needs but would provide support funds for other activities. University administrators responded coolly to the new shop, disliking the competitive challenge it represented for the monopoly the HUB had been enjoying, thereby relegating architecture's shop to a rather sub rosa status. With the turmoil the university was experiencing in the late 1960s and into the '70s, however, coffee shops were seen as an ameliorating influence

*Architecture Hall*

bringing fractious factions harmoniously together, even if only momentarily. Suddenly, the administration reversed its negative coffee shop policy, opening the gates for the innumerable coffee shop satellites scattered about the campus today.

In 1987 the university decided to remedy Architecture Hall's code deficiencies and honor its status as the campus's only major AYPE legacy. Though largely gutted to achieve this goal, the restored Architecture Hall has regained much of the spatial aura of its earlier history. Primarily occupied by the offices, classrooms, and studios of the College's Departments of Architecture and Construction Management, there is also a large auditorium used by many other campus programs. In an upper frieze of the auditorium are engraved the names of some of the notables of the College's faculty and alumni.

*Cunningham Hall*

## 50. Cunningham Hall

*Saunders & Lawton, 1909; The Hastings Group, renovation, 1979*

By curious coincidence, across Stevens Way from AYPE's only remaining permanent building, Architecture Hall, one finds the fair's principal remaining temporary building, Cunningham Hall. A simple case of administrative neglect explains its survival. Though demolition had been its expected fate, it provided space after the fair for a variety of uses including the Bureau of Mines, a Chemistry annex, the Air Force ROTC, and Architecture. In 1975 when the building was finally scheduled for removal, it was suddenly recalled that it had been the AYPE's Women's Building. Renamed to honor the UW graduate and photographer Imogen Cunningham, the building was fully renovated and became the campus Women's Center, with functions that include the Northwest Center for Research on Women and the university's Equal Opportunity Office. Also included is a gallery where work of local women artists is featured.

## 51. Chemistry Library

This is a building with a checkered history, located along Stevens Way just south of Cunningham Hall. Of no particular architectural merit, it housed Seattle's public television facilities and the costume workshop for the

*Chemistry Library*

School of Drama. After those assignments moved elsewhere it assumed its present status as library for the Chemistry Department. Its presence thwarts the potential western alignment of Thurston Lane, postponing an opportunity for establishing an east-west circulation that would tie central campus with the Physics/Astronomy Quad. Such an alignment will no doubt some day continue through the Quad and across Northeast Pacific Street into the Southwest Campus, thus establishing a cross-campus connection between it and the traditional central campus.

## 52. Guthrie Hall   *Bindon, Wright & Partners, 1973*

Built to house the Department of Psychology, and combining administrative, teaching, and research laboratory facilities, Guthrie Hall is located south of Architecture Hall along Stevens Way. The building's design moves away from the skin-taut facades of the 1950s, its brick walls punctuated instead with recessed windows. This robustness of shades and

*Guthrie Hall*

shadows reflects a renewed interest in the building's construction, while not yet demonstrating a concern for contextualism—a trend that then still lay in the future. The building's inner core is a kind of building within a building, composed of a complex of labs for human and animal research. Its name does honor to Edwin R. Guthrie, a member of the psychology faculty for forty-two years who also served eight years as dean of the graduate school. He retired in 1956.

### 53. The Physics/Astronomy Building

*Cesar Pelli and Naramore, Bain, Brady & Johanson, 1994*

That Cesar Pelli, the Connecticut-based architect and American Institute of Architects Gold Medallist, was selected for this major campus project is evidence of a university trend in recent years to seek nationwide for its design consultants. Initially comprised of mostly Seattleites, and then Washingtonians, the university now one finds prominent professionals from many parts of the country doing work on campus. The Electrical Engineering and Chemistry additions are also examples of this practice. Ordinarily, such consultants align themselves with local firms (as in this case), providing themselves with associates familiar with local circumstances. It is generally agreed that the finished results for this project represent a significant campus achievement in both architectural and urban design terms.

The master plan for this corner of the campus envisioned the project as serving the departmental needs of both physics and astronomy. In addition it also was to provide for an eventual circulation linkage between

*The Physics/Astronomy Building*

the central campus via an extended Thurston Lane and a future bridging across Northeast Pacific Street reaching into the Southwest Campus and the comprehensive plan for its redevelopment. The project's small quadrangle moves toward that goal, acting as a knuckle both perceptually and—eventually—functionally to establish that linkage. Located at the northeast entrance to the quad is a twenty-three-foot high sculpture, *Everything that Rises,* by Martin Puryear, one of the country's most celebrated and influential artists today.

Architecturally, here is a complex that fully responds to the current campus policy of contextualism. The building adapts the brick color range and patterning, and the cast stone and terra cotta detailing familiar to upper campus architecture. Note the whimsy of the various physics-inspired inscriptions featured in the exterior trim. Within the building one finds the use of "fritted glass," onto which quasi-crystal patterns have been silk-screened with ceramic-based paints. The Physics /Astronomy Building at last provides these two departments with the state-of-the-art teaching, research, library, and administrative support so seriously lacking in their former central campus locations. Also housed here is the Institute for Nuclear Theory, home for one of the UW's four Nobel Prize winners.

Across the quad is the auditorium and classroom building notable for its distinctive columned arcade. On the building's south facade is a sundial designed by astronomy professor Woodruff Sullivan; his dial is something of a challenge, though instructions tell you how to read for both standard and daylight saving time. Notice also the prominent use of exterior brick patterning, a reference to upper campus design traditions. Under the building's prominent glass cupola visit the atrium with its swinging Foucault pendulum, which demonstrates the rotation of the earth. The building provides a series of auditori-

*Auditorium and classroom building*

ums and other instructional facilities available both to its host departments and other university programs.

The physics/astronomy quad actually is a lid roofing over some twenty underground physics labs, which require a high level of stability to avoid any interference with the accuracy of their processes. The university remains concerned that the future tunneling of Seattle's planned rapid transit route beneath Fifteenth Avenue not weaken that insulation.

## 54. Kincaid Hall  *John Morse and Clayton and Jean Young, 1971*

*Kincaid Hall*

Kincaid Hall shares with Guthrie Hall to the north similarities in materials, color, and forms, and an emphasis on the shades and shadows of wall depth and recessed windows. Although brick was used, the choice in both cases was for color and texture not ordinarily found on this campus. Kincaid's tenant is the department of zoology. The building is named to honor one of the university's "grand old men," Trevor Kincaid, who came to the university in 1895, founded the department, and remained until his retirement in 1942. Noted for his initiative in marine sciences, he established in Friday Harbor, San Juan Islands, the university's Puget Sound Marine Station. When over-harvesting destroyed the native oyster population of Willapa Harbor in southwest Washington, Kincaid successfully introduced a Japanese strain there that revived the industry.

## 55. Benson Hall  *Bindon and Wright, 1966*

*Benson Hall*

Benson Hall is a building of little notability; its somewhat hidden presence across Stevens Way from Kincaid adds to its relative anonymity. Initially the building carried the title of its purpose: Chemical Engineering Building. It was later renamed in honor of the wood-pulp scientist Professor Henry K. Benson, whose research formed an important support for Washington State's timber resource industry. Today it provides facilities for the department of chemical engineering as well as for bioengineering.

*Botany Greenhouse*

## 56. Botany Greenhouse   *1949*

Here is a utilitarian structure and a unit of the botany department.
Originally called the New Botany Greenhouse, it was erected to supple-
ment the old greenhouse built beside Parrington (at that time the Science
Building). Much modernized in recent years and ordinarily little noted, it
recently basked in considerable notoriety when its exotic Devil's Tongue
(*Amorphophallus titanum*) produced a six-foot plant, from seeds planted six
years earlier, whose bloom gave off an unforgettable stench. Not without
reason, this plant in its native Sumatra is called the "corpse flower." In this
century there have been only nine previous flowerings of a Devil's Tongue
plant. This blooming, the first to occur west of St. Louis, attracted some
3,000 visitors.

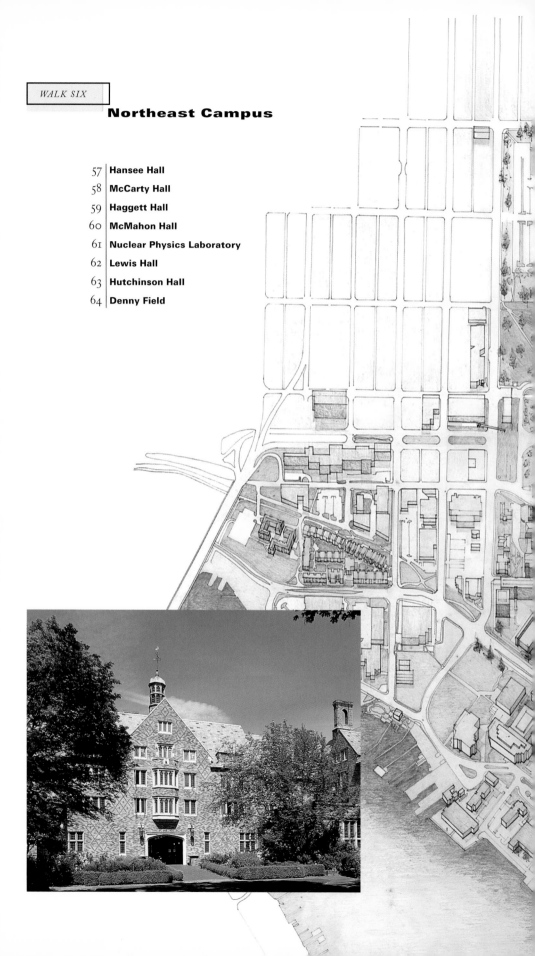

# Northeast Campus

# Dormitory Row

In the initial occupancy of its new site the university spontaneously assigned its northeast corner to an activist role. They placed here the oval Athletic Field and the shed-like combination Armory and Gymnasium just to the north. Later on, however, campus planners determined that this corner of the campus was more appropriate for university-sponsored student housing. It was somewhat removed though not remote from the commercial distractions of "the Ave" and was near the orbit of Greek Row housing due north from the campus across Northeast 45th Street. Likewise, while convenient to Central Campus, it had view-capturing sites on the easterly campus bluffs above Montlake Boulevard. The completion of Hansee Hall in 1936 was the first step in the realization of this area's new designation. World War II delayed further development in the area, but once the campus was returned to peacetime normalcy there followed a surge of additional dormitory construction, which dominates this sixth Walk. Interesting too is the domitories' documentation of social change. What was originally strictly observed gender separation for university dorms began to change in the 1970s so that now all university dorms are coed.

### 57. Hansee Hall   *David J. Myers and John Graham, 1939*

As mentioned earlier, the first dormitory construction on the university's new campus included two dorms, Lewis Hall for men and Clark Hall for women. But thereafter the university made no further efforts in student housing. The policy, at least by inference, was that students were on their own; even those two early dorms had been converted to other uses by the 1930s.

The construction of Hansee Hall signified a university recommitment to a campus housing policy, abetted by the attractions of both Federal (WPA) and state (SERF) emergency funding. The results clearly demonstrate the impact of Ivy-League precedent: plans, forms, and Gothic style evoke the cloistered ambiance and charm of those East coast colleges. Hansee's plan is an elaborate H, each wing having its own identity, with all four linked together at the center where the communal services are located. The wings are elevated to the status of "houses," each honoring a women significant in state and university history: Eliza Ferry Leary, daughter of the first governor of the state of Washington; Catherine V. Blaine, Seattle's first school teacher; Ruth Karr McKee, first woman appointed to the university's board of regents, and Isabella Austin, appointed dean of women in 1960. In l96l, the regents gave the building the overall name of Hansee Hall, honoring Martha Louis Hansee, a turn-of-the-century dean of women. During World War II the dorm was converted to men's housing as a Navy ROTC barracks. Reverting to women's dorms after the war, today both men and women

*Hansee Hall*

occupy it. The south facing court overlooking Denny Field is especially pleasant for its landscaping.

In Hansee's courtyards there are two notable trees. In the westward courtyard is a European mountain ash (*Sorbus aucuparia*), a native of Europe and western Asia, also known as the Rowan tree. In European folklore its wood was believed to be a charm protecting its bearer from witchcraft. The courtyard facing east holds a splendid tulip poplar (*Liriodendron tulipfera*), native to the East coast. Its name comes from its four-lobed leaves resembling a tulip in outline. After the tree has leafed out, the flowers come later, greenish-yellow petals with orange at their base.

## 58. McCarty Hall   *Young, Richardson and Carleton, 1960, 1962*

Honoring Clara McCarty who was granted the university's first collegiate diploma in 1876, McCarty Hall admirably employs the slopes of a descending site with a series of levels that open to the north and east. Its construction was completed in two phases, eventually accommodating some six hundred women, though it is now coed. Architecturally, McCarty's

*McCarty Hall*

distinction lies in its handling of its challenging site, not in its style, which is dryly modern, unlike its pre-war neighbor, Hansee Hall, to the west.

*Haggett Hall*

### 59. Haggett Hall   *Kirk, Wallace, McKinley & Associates, 1963*

Haggett Hall's design documents the next phase in the development of the university's policy on student housing. Responding to student demand, it was phasing out its in loco parentis responsibilities, increasingly transferring to them responsibility for their own lifestyles. Whereas McCarty Hall was originally designed for women only, Haggett Hall edged into a somewhat more flexible arrangement. Composed of two parallel towers—one for men, the other for women—the building contained coed lounges and dining facilities on the connecting ground level. The poured concrete towers were designed to maximize views of the campus lowlands to the east and the Cascades in the distance, and the window orientation in the towers was probably also designed to discourage intratower peeking! Appropriately named in memory of *two* Haggetts, Winifred S., dean of women from 1923 to 1939, and Arthur, from 1917 professor of Greek and later dean of the College of Liberal Arts, Haggett Hall introduced parking for the first time— space for 166 cars on the building's lower levels.

At the southwest corner of Haggett Hall is the twisted form of a corkscrew willow (*Salix matsudana var. tortuosa*), an exotic native of China and Korea.

*McMahon Hall*

**60. McMahon Hall**   *Kirk, Wallace, McKinley & Associates, 1965*

The largest and last of the crescent of dorms built in this eastern area of the
campus is McMahon Hall, a complex geometry of vertically-thrusting
columns with balconies like dresser drawers pulled out and open to the sky;
it has perhaps been unfairly criticized for the poured-concrete brutality of its
construction. Seeking to avoid the impersonal regularity of halls lined by

rooms on either side, the architects in this case tied to encourage a more personalized space by establishing "quads"—four double rooms clustered about a shared lounge. A coed dorm from its beginnings, the building retains single-sex orientation in each quad. Housing 1100 students, McMahon also provides shelter for 180 cars. Its name, like Haggett's, does double duty, memorializing both Edward McMahon, professor of history from 1908 to 1940, and his wife, Theresa McMahon, a teacher of economics and business from 1911 to 1937.

Just south of McMahon Hall on Stevens Way is Gardeners' Vista, which opens to a grand view of Lake Washington and the Cascades. Its creation in 1983 recognized the university's gardening staff and their contribution to the beauties of the campus.

### 61. Nuclear Physics Laboratory  *John Graham, 1965*

Leaving McMahon Hall and moving south brings you to Pend Oreille Road; following it downward to the left one comes to the Nuclear Physics Laboratory. Its somewhat isolated presence is perhaps suggestive of the specialized nature of its university role. The Van de Graaff accelerator and cyclotron housed within are the basis for much of the lab's research in such fields as physics, chemistry, cancer therapy, and nuclear medicine.

*Nuclear Physics Laboratory*

*Lewis Hall*

### 62. Lewis Hall  *Josenhans & Allan, 1899*

Coming to Lewis Hall takes one back to the earliest origins of the campus.
Its construction followed that of the 1895 Denny Hall. Originally intended as
the men's dorm, it and its women's dorm companion, Clark Hall, were completed together in 1899. In both cases they were sited not with any overall
campus plan in mind, but to provide their occupants with views of Lake
Washington and the distant Cascades. Only later when Professor Fuller
established his Oval Plan did they (rather inadvertently) find a place in a
larger scheme of things. Both buildings were named for the famous early
nineteenth-century explorers, Meriwether Lewis in this case (and very
timely in our day, given the great public interest that the explorers are cur-
rently enjoying). Its campus role has been volatile: it was originally a dorm
for fifty men; it bore the name Pierrepont Hall in 1903 for no known reason;
in 1909 it served as a temporary AYPE exhibition building; it became Lewis
Hall again in 1917 and after World War I a women's dorm. It was rebuilt in
1936 to house the School of Communications; today it shelters a cluster of
offices for administration and doctoral students, primarily associated with
the School of Business Administration. The successive remodelings that
those changes represent have managed to obliterate any sense of what the
building's interiors might have been like in those early days. A $25,000
investment by the university when originally built, Lewis and Clark Halls
nevertheless retain with their stolid brick-clad personalities a certain digni-
fied and respected campus role.

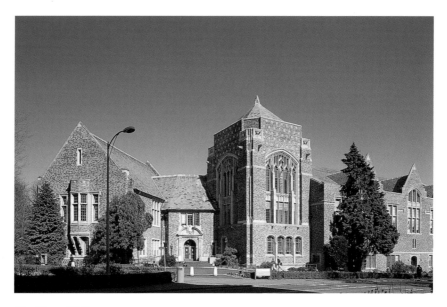

*Hutchinson Hall*

### 63. Hutchinson Hall   *Bebb and Gould, 1927*

This building was originally designed as the Women's Gymnasium. It remained so until 1984, when the women moved into gym facilities on lower campus, leaving the building to become the headquarters for the School of Drama. This accounts for the presence of some of the spatial qualities not ordinarily associated with drama (like a swimming pool, still active) and a large ball court (now divided into a variety of classrooms). Because of its upper campus location and its date, Collegiate Gothic ruled, and in this case quite grandly. Hutchinson's central tower serves as a kind of sentinel announcing central campus if one approaches it on Stevens Way coming from the north. That role is now reinforced by its partner due west, Balmer's new SEEC tower. The gabled roof profile, the traditional brick cladding, the handsome cast stone trim of doors and windows, and the extensive facade paralleling Stevens Way all give Hutchinson Hall considerable visual clout.

### 64. Denny Field

A spatial remnant from the campus' earliest days, Denny Field remains a generous open space. In the distant past it was the university's principal playing field, the theater of some of the university's early football successes. The men left behind the wood-frame bleachers, fencing, and the old

*Denny Field*

nearby gymnasium when they and their games moved south to the new lower campus stadium and pavilion in 1928. The field then served as a women's gym facility until they too moved on; it remains today a resource for less programmed, more spontaneous field sports. Its volleyball and basketball courts and a fringe of tennis courts are especially active now that the surrounding area has developed as a student residential area.

## East-Central Campus

Beginning to the north with the liberal arts offices of Padelford Hall, the functional tilt of this campus sector soon melds into the sciences, with a variety of academic and service buildings accommodating those needs. With some exception, there are fewer pretensions here for ceremonial architecture—function has been given priority over form. As compensation, many occupants of these heights share the benefits of easterly vistas: athletics and parking in the foreground, followed by the flatlands of Lake Washington, then the housing and institutions of Laurelhurst, and finally the distant Cascades.

### 65. Padelford Hall   *Walker/McGough, 1967*

In the professional architectural press of the day, the 1958-62 Ezra Stiles and Morse Colleges designed by Eero Saarinen at Yale University were well publicized; clearly their distinctively quirky plans were the inspiration for that of Padelford Hall. The site's natural topography made it the logical location in 1909 for the Alaska-Yukon-Pacific Exposition's (AYPE) outdoor amphitheater bowl, into which Padelford Hall now nests comfortably. The bowl's lower levels are out of sight and have been filled in with a parking garage. The Hall honors Frederick M. Padelford, one of the university's grand old men, who arrived on campus in 1901 and remained here as professor of English, departmental chairman, and finally Graduate School

*Padelford Hall*

dean, a post he held until his death in 1942. Assigned to a wide range of liberal arts administrative and faculty offices, Padelford Hall admittedly poses a challenge for those unfamiliar with its plan's internal convolutions. Nevertheless it provides many an office with splendid territorial views; housed within are such departmental members as English, comparative literature, romance languages, mathematics, linguistics, and the Mathematics Research Library.

### 66. Hall Health Center

*A. H. Albertson, Wilson & Richardson, 1936; Cummings Associates, east wing, 1978*

Just south of Padelford is Hall Health Center, whose name honors David C. Hall, from 1908 to 1948 the university's health officer as well as its professor of hygiene. Hall was certainly a forebear of today's health activists—his advocacy and his participation as a runner, hiker and handballer surely anticipated today's joggers and their ilk. The building, facing Stevens Way, is a subdued expression of the Collegiate Gothic style and screens off—not unsuitably—the brutal baldness of its much later poured concrete east wing addition.

*Hall Health Center*

*Faculty Center*

### 67. Faculty Center

*Paul Hayden Kirk & Associates and Victor Steinbrueck, 1960*

In exclamatory contrast to the Health Center is its neighbor to the south, the Faculty Center. It was designed by an architectural firm that emerged in the postwar years with a record of creative residential projects, demonstrating in its work a unique recognition of the Pacific Northwest's regionalism. Though recognized as the premier architectural evidence on campus of the international style, the Faculty Center is also an interpretation in steel and glass of the spirit of the firm's wood-frame residential work: its structural module of verticals and horizontals, the spatial flow of its interiors, and the generous window area opening to near and distant vistas. There is no hint here of the contextualism later advocated by the university, yet its some-what independent site softens any intrusiveness. Below the pedestrian ramp leading up to the entrance, note the stone Corinthian capital, a rem-nant from the destruction of Seattle's old downtown post office.

This location had in AYPE days been the site of the Hoo-Hoo House, a gathering place for the visiting lumbermen during the fair and the work of the noted local architect Ellsworth Storey. After the fair it became the University Faculty Club, until its destruction in 1959. The only remnants of that earlier history can be found in some of the rough-hewn wood paneling in the downstairs bar, some Oriental rugs, and its fireplace andirons. Also note the gold sculpture panels of the main-lounge fireplace; their sculptor was the art school's Everett DuPen.

## 68. Fluke Hall (Washington Technology Center)

*Naramore, Bain, Brady & Johanson, 1990*

One gets a very good view from the Faculty Center's east windows of Fluke Hall, so called because of a major financial donation by the Fluke family; it memorializes John M. Fluke, Sr. In the chambers of the 1983 legislature there was considerable enthusiasm for state-sponsored technology initiatives to reinforce the state's economy. One of the results was the funding for this building, designed as a center for seeking out such commercially promising technology and hastening it to the marketplace. The building's design is responsive to the evolving nature of its exploratory and somewhat unpredictable program needs. The "permanent" administrative functions of the Center are housed in brick-clad construction reminiscent of the upper campus, and the building nestles into the site's steep westerly slopes. The exploratory activities of the Center, which by their very nature are more uncertain and elusive as to their future spatial requirements, are sited to the east; the site in that direction lending itself to a variety of expansions. Here the building's construction is modularized and sheathed with corrugated metal panels for easy expansion. Among the spin-offs from the Center's activities have been such additions to Washington's technology base as the Human Genome Center, the Center for Nanotechnology, and Microvision.

*Fluke Hall*

*Engineering Library*

*Loew Hall*

## 69. Engineering Library and Loew Hall

*Fred Bassetti & Company, 1969*

These two buildings were designed as an ensemble; they share a small quad. Each, however, has its own identity that responds to the different roles they play in engineering education—one a library, the other for administration and classroom purposes; one a cube as a kind of centerpiece building to the quad's north, the other an elongated more subdued companion to the south, its cantilevered top floor establishing the quad's southern wall. Both have distinctive eyebrow windows. The architect was noted for his interest in brick for both its functional and decorative potentials and that enthusiasm is fulsomely demonstrated here. Loew Hall's name honors Engineering Professor Edgar A. Loew and his long university tenure from 1909 until retirement as dean of his College in 1948. The offices of the College of Engineering are located here as well as classrooms and other administrative facilities.

## 70. Mechanical Engineering Building and Engineering Annex

**Mechanical Engineering Building**   *Carlson, Elley & Grevstad, 1959*
**Engineering Annex**   *1909*

This dry 1950s building parallels Stevens Way, serving as a visual foil for its much earlier annex, a leftover from the AYPE. Today both serve the teaching, research, and administrative needs of the department of mechanical

*Mechanical Engineering and Engineering Annex*

engineering and the industrial engineering program. At the time of the fair this site was occupied by two parallel structures named Machinery Hall, but the building closest to Stevens Way was torn down to make way for the present building. Its more utilitarian rear half, with its heavy timber-frame construction, still stands—a lingering reminder of the special place the fair had in the history of the campus.

**71. More Hall**   *Bebb and Jones, Leonard Bindon, Associates, 1946*

Both the Mechanical Engineering Building and More Hall remind us that the Collegiate Gothic stylistic dictates of upper campus did not extend to construction on lower campus. These two buildings, the latter dedicated

*More Hall*

to the program needs of the Department of Civil and Environmental Engineering, chose to go their own way and thus suffer from the postwar design uncertainties of the 1940s and 1950s. Professor Charles C. More, for whom the building is named, was another long-tenured faculty member, joining the university in 1900 when the department's discipline was called structural engineering and remaining until 1949. Framing the entrance is a series of cast-aluminum roundels, the 1947 work of Dudley Pratt.

At More Hall's west end facing Stevens Way is another sculptural remnant from the AYPE, this one by Finn H. Frolich—a bronze bust of James J. Hill of Pacific Northwest railroading fame. Much credit is due him for the early railroads connecting Seattle to the rest of the nation, which the fair recognized with this statue.

## 72. Nuclear Reactor Building

*Gene Zema, Wendell Lovett, and Daniel Streissguth, 1961*

The robust poured-concrete forms of this , designed to house the university's Nuclear Reactor, surely suggest the protective, sheltering role of the building. This is one of those rare occasions when members of the Architecture faculty, Lovett and Streissguth, were granted a university commission. The reactor's original function has been superceded by more

*Nuclear Reactor Building*

advanced technology, and as a result it awaits decommissioning, the funding for which remains elusive. The building faces an uncertain future.

## 73. Power Plant

*Howard & Galloway, 1909; Bouillon Christofferson and Parsons Brinckerhof, renovation, 1999–2000*

By 1903 the university had built its first power plant, in a location that is under today's Suzzallo Library. It even remained in place during the AYPE in a location hidden behind an encircling screen of display buildings. A new plant was built in 1909 as part of the AYPE construction in a location convenient for coal deliveries, just above the railroad tracks and due east of the Engineering Annex. Over the years it has been successively remodeled and extended to accommodate increasing heating and cooling load demands as the campus developed and changes in technology occurred. Recently, because of seismic concerns, a new unitary steel stack replaced the original brick stack. A substantial addition to the south was also recently constructed.

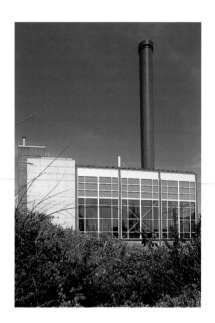

*Power Plant*

## 74. Roberts Hall   *Bebb and Gould, 1921; Duarte Bryant, renovation, 1988*

We return to the Collegiate Gothic style with this handsome building, which was originally designed to house the pragmatic needs of the College of Mines. One of the college's initial programs was in ceramic engineering, at a time when terra cotta was a popular architectural finish material; Seattle's downtown is noted for its many buildings that are products of that enthusiasm. An early work of Bebb and Gould's campus career, today it serves the department of materials science and engineering. The building was impressively remodeled recently. Professor Milnor Roberts, for whom the building was named, was another of the university's venerable early faculty personalities, with a forty-six-year record here beginning in 1901. A mining engineer, he was dean of his college and a generous donor to the university.

*Roberts Hall*

Until his death he lived in his home just across from the campus on Fifteenth Street, since destroyed. Over the Roberts Hall entrance is an interesting cartouche, surmounted by a fierce winged lion.

### 75. Mueller Hall   *Ralph Anderson; Koch Durante, 1986*

Anxious to retain the prominence and vista enjoyed by Roberts Hall but facing expansion needs, the university decided to burrow into Roberts rather than build on the open space between it and Stevens. Thus Mueller Hall does nothing to interrupt Roberts Hall's setback visibility—its spaces

*Mueller Hall*

are located under the cover of the entrance terrace and lawn approaching Roberts Hall. Mueller's interiors open out to the space and light of their own somewhat hidden, sunken and paved quad. This is significant evidence of the priority that the university has in more recent decades exercised in the preservation and enhancement of the urban design of the campus. James I. Mueller, for whom the hall is named, was on the faculty from 1949 to 1973, a professor of mining and metallurgical and ceramic engineering and for three years the departmental chairman.

## 76. Wilcox Hall and Wilson Ceramic Laboratory

**Wilson Ceramic Laboratory**  *Paul Thiry, 1946*
**Wilcox Hall**  *McClure & Atkinson, 1963*

This building, directly bridged to Roberts Hall, serves a variety of engineering programs under the aegis of the College of Engineering. Its name honors Elgin Roscoe Wilcox, onetime head of the department of general engineering, who was at the university from 1920 to 1962. Due west is a neighbor, Wilson Ceramic Laboratory, honoring Hewitt Wilson, professor of ceramic engineering, who guided the development of the department from 1919 to 1939. With the planned demolition of the 1948 Electrical Engineering Building, the lab will stand as the only building on campus designed by Paul Thiry, one of the university's most distinguished architectural graduates.

*Wilcox Hall and Wilson Ceramic Laboratory*

*Triangle Parking Garage*

## 77. Triangle Parking Garage

*Bumgardner Architects; SWA, landscape architect, 1985*

When the construction sign was put up on Montlake Boulevard to announce the Triangle Parking Garage, the community was in uproar. How dare the university desecrate Rainier Vista with a parking garage? Welcoming this demonstration of the community's commitment to aesthetics, the university quickly amended its sign to read *underground* garage. The above-ground aspect of the project concerned the treatment of the landscape, which went through considerable review in efforts to enhance appropriately this major visual gateway from the south into the campus. Though some people have reservations about the monoculture evergreen groves framing both sides of the vista, on the whole the simplicity (and economy) of the radiating English ivy beds, the steps with their flanking walls, and the plane of a great circular planting bed suitably celebrate Rainier Vista—as it visually sweeps up into Central Plaza or, in reverse, on toward Mount Rainier.

# West-Central Campus

## *Where the Campus Begins Its Westward Ho*

Originally, Fifteenth Avenue Northeast had demarcated the west edge of the campus, but the university's revised campus plan of 1948 revealed that even the generous proportions of the original 1895 campus were insufficient to absorb the university's continuing postwar expansion. The 1948 plan recommended as a first priority a campus expansion westward from Fifteenth Avenue into what was known as the Northlake area. The Federal Government's Urban Renewal Program enabled the acquisition of the land—an addition of thirty-four acres, extending the campus south from Forty-first Street to Portage Bay and west to the University Bridge and its connections. It is the evolution of this new university area that is central to what one finds on this Walk.

### 78. Campus Parkway  *1953*

In the 1920s President Suzzallo dreamed of a grand ceremonial route leading from the west and the north end of University Bridge to the university campus. Difficult to achieve because of the intervening extant residential and commercial properties, it was nevertheless an idea that was given additional clout by its inclusion in the 1948 Campus Plan. Its completion in 1953 brought University Bridge traffic to the campus, but abruptly so, with only a hint of panache and with no destination clearly established. Cluttered with utility poles and wires, it is unfortunately aligned visually with the new

*Campus Parkway*

skylit portion of the Henry's addition, which inauspiciously blurs the parkway's visual axis on the George Washington statue and Suzzallo Library's façade beyond. At the parkway's western end the irregular plantings of trees (remnants of a 1961 international forestry conference) add to a general dishevelment that does violence to the ambitions Suzzallo had. This is a parkway leading nowhere.

### 79. Schmitz Hall   *Waldron & Pomeroy, 1970*

Schmitz Hall, one of the first new buildings marking the university's leap to the west, recognizes the presidency from 1952 to 1958 of Henry Schmitz. Sited on its own reinforced concrete podium, Schmitz Hall features a cantilevered succession of floors, which create strong patterns of shades and shadows. It includes such facilities as the university registrar, office of minority affairs, office of student affairs, the student counseling center, and financial aid office. As you travel over Schmitz's connecting pedestrian bridge from Central Campus, on one landing you see the bronze sculpture by Philip Levine, *Dancer with a Flat Hat*, helpfully pointing out the correct route.

*Schmitz Hall*

*Playhouse Theater*

### 80. Playhouse Theater

*Arthur C. Loveless, 1931; Nelsen, Sabin & Varey, renovation, 1968*

Originally built for a privately owned Seattle repertory theater, this building was designed by Loveless, a noted Seattle architect better known for his upscale residential commissions. The university acquired it in 1951. Loveless' taste for English country houses is evident in the theater, with its low-slung picturesque gabled roofs, brick facades, and charming entry court. Most of these features were lost in the 1968 expansion and remodeling. The playhouse is one of the theaters operated by the School of Drama for student performances. The internationally noted Seattle painter, the late Mark Toby, did two mosaic murals on either side of the entry doors.

### 81. Condon Hall

*Mitchell/Giurgola Associates; Joyce, Copeland, Vaughan & Nordfors, 1973*

*Condon Hall*

This is the second building on campus named to honor John T. Condon, who served on the faculty from 1899 to 1926 and was the School of Law's first dean. The first Condon Hall was one of those surrounding the Liberal Arts Quad, now Gowen Hall, but after this new building's completion his name was transferred to it along with its role as home of the law school. It was the first time the university had conducted a nation-wide search for its architect, choosing an AIA Gold Medallist firm from Philadelphia for the project. Condon provides classrooms, offices, and an extensive law library. The school's transition to the new building, however, has been an unhappy one. Students and faculty, accustomed to the center-campus Collegiate Gothic ambiance of its former quarters, took unkindly to the stark and rather forbidding poured-concrete environs of their new digs. But the university has scheduled a new law school building to be constructed shortly on the central campus, with a site that defines the north edge of Campus Green.

### 82. Terry-Lander Halls  *Young, Richardson, Carleton & Detlie, 1953, 1957*

After the 1939 completion of Hansee Hall the university did not take on any new construction for student housing, depending instead on Greek Row, a few private living organizations, and students' own housing initiatives to fill the void. With the growth of the student population after the war and federal funding assistance, the university renewed its interest in housing. Terry and then Lander Halls were the first results, both designed as men's dorms. Terry Hall, the more westerly of the two, was named for Charles C. Terry, one of those who had joined to make the land donation for the university's first campus. Lander Hall honors Judge Edward Lander, who with Terry and Arthur and Mary Denny, donated the ten-acre downtown site. Today both dorms are coeducational. Each is conventional in plan and elevation, representative of the cautious modernism exercised in campus areas beyond the predominantly Collegiate Gothic central campus.

*Terry-Lander Halls*

*Commodore-Duchess Apartments*

### 83. Commodore-Duchess Apartments   *Earl Roberts, 1929–1930;*
*Stickney & Murphy, renovation, 1997*

These identical apartments were built separately by private owners for
residential purposes. In 1960 when the university acquired them for married
student housing, they were internally joined. Both were recently rehabilitated to satisfy code requirements and occupant expectations.

### 84. Gould Hall and Community Design Center
*Daniel Streissguth and Gene Zema, 1971*

This Walk, focused on buildings beyond the confines of the original campus, includes several poured-concrete behemoths: Schmitz Hall, then Gould
Hall, with Condon Hall soon to follow. Gould Hall was built to accommodate
the bulk of activities associated with the College of Architecture and Urban
Planning. Carl F. Gould, for whom the building is named, was the university's "unofficial architect," the founder of the architecture program in 1914,
and director of that program for many years. Other built environmental disciplines have since been added, so that today the college is composed of
four departments: architecture, construction management, landscape architecture, and urban design and planning, as well as a number of more specialized subgroups.

The architects for Gould represented an unusual team, as one of
them, Streissguth, was a member of the Architecture faculty—an arrange-

ment usually avoided by the university administration in its selection of design professionals. His colleague for this project, Gene Zema, built a notable mostly residential design reputation in the '50s and '60s. Their collaboration resulted in a very dramatic multi-storied central atrium around which the successive floors of the building range. The rationale behind this configuration lay in the college's desire for unity amongst the various departments. Included are studios, classrooms, a woodshop, computer labs, a library, and various departmental and faculty offices. The coffee shop at the atrium's east end contributes substantially to that communal cohesion. Gould's somewhat forbidding exterior belies a much more humane internal lifestyle. From Fifteenth Avenue just south of Gould Hall is a 1990 student design/build garden court, redesigned in 1997 to memorialize Gordon Varey, dean of the College of Architecture and Urban Planning from 1982 to 1992, who died tragically in an airplane accident.

Due west and across University Way from Gould Hall is a little high-tech building designed by the architect Barnett Schorr. Originally built to house a restaurant called Man Bites Dog, it was later acquired by the university and serves as the department of architecture's community design center. It houses design studios. At its west end is the 1998 Garden of Eatin, a handicapped-accessible environment designed and built by landscape architecture undergraduate students, emphasizing the use of edible plant materials.

*Gould Hall*

*Ethnic Cultural Center*

*Child Care Center*

## 85. Ethnic Cultural Center and Child Care Center

**Ethnic Cultural Center**  *Benjamin McAdoo & Company, 1971*
**Child Care Center**  *Meng Associates, 1997*

Two blocks due west of Gould is a block of low-rise buildings, documenting
an important expansion of university responsibility for its academic community. The Ethnic Cultural Center, with its distinctive sawtooth roof line,

offers various facilities and services for the minority student population, including multi-purpose rooms, kitchens, offices, and equipment rooms. For similar reasons, commitments were also extended to those in the university community with children, which resulted in the construction of the Child Care Center, the facilities of which are available to some forty-four children of university faculty and staff.

## 86. Henderson Hall

*Bumgardner Partnership, renovation, 1967; Olson Sundberg, addition, 1987*

The west end of this building was originally built as a commercial ware-house for storage, but after its acquisition by the university around 1950 it was remodeled on two different occasions as facilities for the applied physics lab. The first remodeling made considerable changes within the building but only modest efforts toward relieving the external visual evidence of its warehouse origins. The more ambitious second remodeling included an addition, which offered the architects considerably greater design opportunities, which they successfully exploited. The lab played a significant research role during World War II, and it is one of only four such labs affiliated with the U.S. Navy. Its offices, research, library, and development activities are the jurisdiction of the College of Ocean and Fishery Sciences. At the time of the founding of the lab, Joseph E. Henderson, a physics professor at the university from 1943 to 1969, was named its first director. The building was subsequently named after him.

*Henderson Hall*

*Mercer Hall*

### 87. Mercer Hall   *Royal A. McClure & Co., 1970*

After the rash of dormitory construction fully occupied the northeast ridge
of the campus, the university began placing student-housing facilities on its
newly acquired westerly properties. Mercer Hall's name honors a Seattle
pioneer, Asa S. Mercer, who taught at the university and was its temporary
president from 1861 to 1863. His fame in part was based on his trip east to
bring back to Seattle a group of women known as the Mercer Girls, who
subsequently found local husbands and often became the town's social
matriarchs. Like the other university dorms, Mercer is coeducational, housing 250 students in its two hip-roofed, four-story, brick-clad structures.

Mercer Hall is bordered on the south by the Burke-Gilman Trail, a
former railroad line that linked downtown Seattle to the north and eastern
areas of the region and that once delivered coal to the university's Power
Plant. Its curved tracks—originating in the west and sweeping north along
the east edge of the central campus, paralleling Montlake Boulevard before
moving east toward Lake Washington, Lake Sammamish, and beyond—
played an important part in shaping the campus. Since its abandonment by
the railroad it has been landscaped and converted to an important and
much admired pedestrian, jogging, and bicycle trail.

## 88. Stevens Court

**Phase 1** *Michael /Lakeman and Mithun Partners, 1969*
**Phase 2** *Mithun Partners, 1993*

Stevens Court, named for Isaac I. Stevens, the first territorial governor of the state and an early protagonist in the establishment of the university, is located south of the Burke-Gilman Trail. Its design departs from the higher density of the other housing units in the university's dormitory system. Composed of a series of free-standing units informally grouped about landscaped interior courtyards, the buildings in the westerly portion of the site feature stucco and brick with gabled roofs, while those to the east are three-storied, shingle-walled, and flat-roofed. Together they provide their 500 coeducational student occupants with low-density dormitory facilities with a residential ambiance.

*Stevens Court*

# East Campus

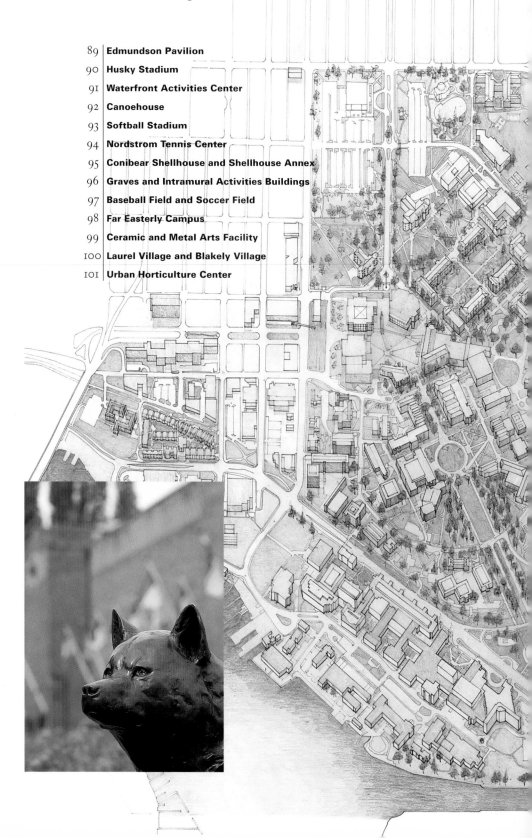

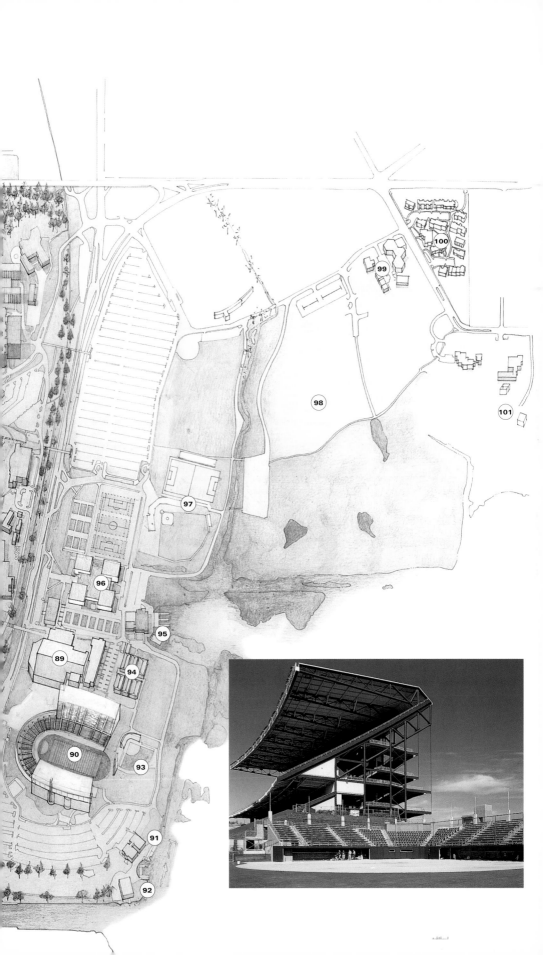

Much of what you see today on your East Campus walk sits on land once covered by the waters of Union Bay, an adjunct of Lake Washington. Until well after the Alaska-Yukon-Pacific Exposition (AYPE) of 1909 the lakeshore was but a short distance in some places from the northward sweep of the railroad line, which provided a sharply defined east edge to the campus. In 1917 the Lake Washington Ship Canal was completed, uniting Lake Union to the west with Lake Washington to the east, and—most tellingly for lake-edge property owners, including the university—lowering Lake Washington by 8.8 feet. In the case of the university fill from dredging added some 100 additional acres to the campus. Subsequent sanitary filling (a euphemism for garbage dump) further expanded the potential for development. Although unstable subsoil conditions prevented construction in some places, such land nevertheless remained ideal for recreation fields, arboretums, and parking, providing the university the luxury of conveniently located acres for such land-consuming purposes.

### 89. Edmundson Pavilion

*Bebb and Gould, 1928; Bebb and Jones, 1939; John Morris & Associates, 1969; Decker, Barnes, Bobbs, Fukui, 1980; Loschky, Marquardt & Nesholm, 2000*

*Edmundson Pavilion*

Certain projects on campus have been paid for not by the university nor by donors but by student-assessed funds. This is especially true of athletic facilities and Edmundson Pavilion is an early example. Clarence S. "Hec" Edmundson was a much venerated figure in the men's physical education program at the university in the years 1920 to 1954. The pavilion was designed principally as the venue for the Huskies' basketball teams. In 1939 a swimming pool was added to the building. More recently, to achieve parity between men's and women's athletic facilities, an important new gymnasium and other additions were made to the pavilion. Presently the original structure is undergoing a thorough rehabilitation and seismic retrofitting for reopening in the new millennium. Until 1998 the pavilion had for many years been the setting for the university's graduation exercises—the

*Edmundson Pavilion, details*

decorations for those occasions gave the space surprising and colorful éclat. The growing number of graduates required that the administration move graduation exercises into the stadium in 1998. So far the skies have remained friendly.

## 90. Husky Stadium

*Bebb and Gould, 1920 and 1937; George Wellington Stoddard and Associates, addition, 1950; Skilling Ward Magnusson Barkshire, engineers, with NBBJ, architect, addition, 1988*

The history of the stadium, whose bulk dominates the campus' lake frontage, started conventionally enough but more recently achieved an unexpected notoriety. Like the Edmundson Pavilion, the stadium was financed in part by student fees, and augmented in this case by the sale of advance seating and plaques. Street level entries led into the stadium's poured-concrete stands, whose successive levels stepped down to the field below. At the east end the stadium opened to the lakefront and beyond that to distant views of Lake Washington and the Cascades—a truly noble setting for the huge audiences the stadium attracted. By 1937 further development added more bleachers, a headhouse, ticket office, concessions, broadcast and public-address systems, and spotlights. Additional seats and a roof for the south stands, built in 1950 again with ASUW funds and considered something of an engineering achievement at the time of construction, raised the presence of the stadium dramatically skyward.

Then in the latter 1980s construction began on new seats and a roof for the north stands, to match those of the south as well as generally to upgrade existing facilities at ground level. But during its construction the structural steel framing for the north stands failed, triggering a collapse that reduced it to a bizarre and dangerous tangle of twisted steel, which one

*Husky Stadium*

wag called "the best piece of modern sculpture on campus." Fortunately, no lives were lost, and the project was completed in time for the opening of the 1998 football season. It is here that the university graduation exercises since 1988 have taken place, a tradition that is uneasily dependent for its success on the caprices of the Northwest climate.

### 91. Waterfront Activities Center   *Donald J. Foote, 1976*

One of the most popular buildings on campus for special meetings and social events is the Waterfront Activities Center. It not only accommodates storage and administration requirements for a range of recreational water sports such as sailing, canoeing, and kayaking, but it also contains upper-floor rooms and decks overlooking Union Bay and the lake and mountains beyond, which are ideal for meetings, special events, and socializing. The center is a busy place, especially during more salubrious months of the year when its boats and canoes, docks, floats, and piers are available, or in the fall for those who come by boat to see the games. The center's rather residential scale and architecture meld comfortably with the visual pleasures of its waterfront site.

### 92. Canoehouse   *L. E. Gregory, engineer, 1918*

The canoehouse is not only on the state's list of historic buildings but is surprisingly the only campus building listed on the National Register of

*Waterfront Activities Center*

*Canoehouse*

Historic Places. It was originally built during World War I as a hangar for seaplanes of the Aviation Training Corps; they never arrived, however, and the building was never used as a hangar. Instead, it became the university's shellhouse, supporting its nationally acclaimed rowing crews. After more adequate facilities were built for the crew, the building was converted to use as a boathouse for the Husky Sailing Club. Rehabilitated in recent years, the timber-framed and shingled canoehouse retains much of the personality of its early days.

Only a short way westward from the canoehouse is the Climbing Rock, designed by the architects Anderson & Bell in 1974. Perhaps seen deservedly by some as a successful sculptural work, it was in reality built for rock-climbing enthusiasts.

### 93.  Softball Stadium    *Loschky, Marquardt & Nesholm, 1997*

Here is another campus development that reflects the changing mores and legal requirements of our time. This new Women's Softball Field reflects efforts to bring the standards of women's athletic facilities on par with men's.

*Softball Stadium*

## 94. Nordstrom Tennis Center   *The McKinley Architects, 1987*

*Nordstrom Tennis Center*

In a climate such as Seattle's, the failure to provide year-round facilities for tennis players severely handicapped the university teams. The Nordstrom family financed this handsome tennis center to correct that problem. In it one finds six courts, ancillary locker and shower rooms for both the men's and women's teams, as well as meeting rooms, spectator facilities, and a lobby. It is a story of rags to riches for the university's tennis community.

## 95. Conibear Shellhouse and Shellhouse Annex

**Conibear Shellhouse**   *Bebb and Jones, 1949*
**Shellhouse Annex**   *Kramer, Chin & Mayo; The Miller/Hull Partnership, 1993*

The Conibear Shellhouse is architecturally of little distinction, though it serves adequately to shelter the rowing shells of the university crew. Originally it also housed the crew, but in more recent years it has been converted to more versatile purposes: dining facilities and the administrative

*Conibear Shellhouse*

*Conibear Shellhouse and Annex*

and academic advising offices for all athletic programs of the university. Its name honors the memory of Hiram Conibear, who began serving the university as a football trainer and track coach but by 1907 had found his true genius in a sport for which he had no previous experience, rowing. His probing analysis of the sport—both in its physiological and psychological demands for success—resulted in the creation of the Huskies' "Conibear Stroke." This secret weapon brought the crew and the university winnings at a national and international level, crowned by the gold in the 1936 Berlin Olympics. Conibear's honors should be shared with George Pocock, whom Conibear brought to the university in 1912. As an English-born boat builder, Pocock designed and built shells that became the lightest and fastest in the world. The Conibear/Pocock duo turned Seattle and the University of Washington into a world class rowing center—UW graduates have become rowing coaches around the world.

Architecturally, the shellhouse annex has a somewhat more interesting history. It was built to house the crew coaches' launches and other elements of the crew's flotilla. Because its curved roof form is identical to that of the long demolished 1906 ASUW canoehouse, one would presume the architects of the new building were inspired by it. Yet, on inquiry, it transpires that they were not familiar with that precedent nor had they seen photographs; it seems that with their Annex they subliminally created a mirroring of the past, linking it with the present!

### 96. The Graves and Intramural Activities Buildings

*Robert Billsbrough Price Associates, 1963, 1968*

Both of these buildings were designed by the same architect in close proximity to one another and serving the intercollegiate and intramural athletic programs of the university. The Graves Building, named for Dorsett "Tubby" Graves, whose university career lasted from 1922 to 1947, houses the administrative offices of the university's athletic programs. Its neighbor, the Intramural Activities Building, provides coeducational and intramural support with its four gymnasiums, a swimming pool, and other specialized features, as well as offices for students and a variety of intramural team-related associations.

*Graves Building*

*Intramural Activities Building*

*Baseball Field*

## 97. Baseball Field and Soccer Field   *Stanley A. Smith, 2000*

*Soccer Field*

Both of these fields are presently in a state of transition. The Baseball Field had formerly been located rather inconveniently in the furthermost northeast corner of the campus, but the university's baseball teams have now enjoyed two seasons in their present and far more accessible new location. It however is still a field in progress, the present temporary bleachers serving until funds are raised for permanent arrangements.

As for the soccer field, previously there had been no such university facility, a reflection of this sport's earlier lowly status. In recent years, however, that has changed, resulting in the need for appropriate facilities, this new field being the consequence. Like baseball, soccer looks forward to the future funding of a permanent soccer stadium.

## 98  Far Easterly Campus

This great open space roughly north of the Intramural Activities Building and east of Montlake Boulevard became after the lowering of the lake level a sanitary fill area, much of it unsuitable for construction. In the early 1960s filling was halted and the university began efforts to make it a more presentable and useful place. In addition to parking, portions were assigned to recreational use, thus accounting for the new baseball and soccer fields and, farther north, for the golf driving range and an intramural sports field. But the more easterly area was devoted to open space and a wildlife area, a concept supported by the university, community groups, and individuals. Studies revealed that due to the subsoil conditions the university could expect further settlement to take place, with ponds evolving, and the spontaneous influx of native plant materials and various birds and animal species. Uncertain of what kinds of plant materials could survive there, given the nature of its subsoil history, the university established programs to investigate. The Urban Horticulture Center is presently carrying out various experimental research and preservation efforts to understand and nurture this unique habitat.

Some of the land to the east beyond the fill area is buildable, thus, one finds there certain campus service facilities—such as environmental safety and corp yards—and others more central to key university objectives including:

### 99. Ceramic and Metal Arts Facility   *Carlson Architects, 1969*

This group of structures is primarily composed of three hexagonal low-rise modular units joined together to form in plan a shallow arc. The units

*Ceramic and Metal Arts Facility*

were intended as a "temporary" arrangement, but like all such campus construction, they have a remarkable tenacity. The facility includes a foundry, sculpture and welding studio, and ceramic kilns—technologies of the fire arts and all aspects of the teaching programs of the School of Art where metals and ceramics are the facility's specialized media. The adjoining fenced utilitarian yards and their somewhat rumpled contents add to the creative aura that surrounds the place.

### 100. Laurel Village and Blakely Village

*Michael /Lakeman, 1982*

These two residential villages, designed in a similar fashion by the architectural firm Michael/Lakeman for the housing of married students and their families. Laurel Village across the street from the fire arts buildings was built to provide shelter in a grouping of two-story units for a total of eighty families. Included also are community and childcare centers, the latter accommodating the children of student residents of the village and some outsiders.

The second of these villages, Blakely Village, completed the same year, is farther north above the University Village shopping center. It provides eighty-four apartments as well as a community center forits residents.

*Laurel Village*

*Urban Horticulture Center*

### 101.   **Urban Horticulture Center**   *Jones and Jones, 1962–1989*

This center is an example of the importance that private donations have
come to represent in the university's more recent history, for the five different construction projects that make up this complex were all funded by
such donations. Together they also represent an innovation in that they
house a university program dedicated to the study of plants and ecosys-
tems in urban landscapes. The facilities themselves are varied, including an
interesting conservatory (both structure and contents), conference facilities,
and the Elisabeth C. Miller Horticulture Library. The buildings are all
designed and scaled to be compatible with the residential district that the
Center borders., the central buildings clustering about an attractive internal
court. The grounds surrounding the complex also demonstrate a range of
plant materials that are congenial in urban environments as well as having
potential for innovative applications.

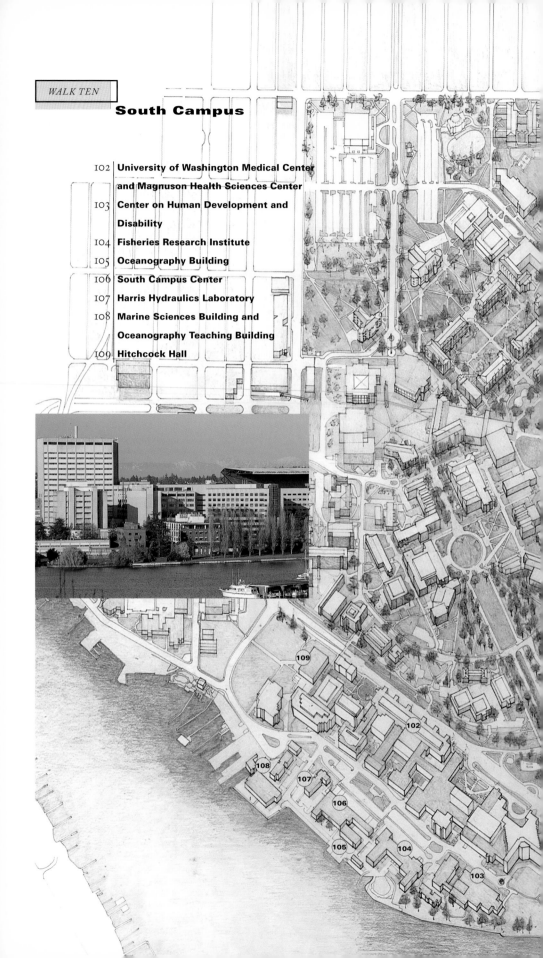

# *Where the University Golf Course Used to Be*

Before World War II there was a nine-hole golf course handsomely located paralleling Northeast Pacific Street to the north and south above the shore of Portage Bay and the canal. Other university facilities, often water-related like Fisheries and Oceanography, had also found places along the shore. The open golf-course site proved ideal, however, for the location of the medical school. Most of the area's former spaciousness has now disappeared with the high-density development brought by the postwar years.

### 102. University of Washington Medical Center and Magnuson Health Sciences Center

*Naramore, Bain, Brady & Johanson, 1948–1950; NBBJ, 1960, 1965, 1972; Caudill Rowlett Scott, 1985; MBT Associates and TRA, 1995*

Although as early as 1884 the university's Board of Regents expressed interest in adding a medical school to its agenda, resistance by the local medical profession and indifference on the part of the faculty and state legislature meant that for years Washingtonians desiring medical careers were required to go elsewhere for their education. When, however, after World War II the state legislature gave the university authority to develop the new medical school, it did so with the avowed intention that it be top-rank. To a remarkable extent it succeeded. Washington and the university are deservedly proud of the splendid record of achievement that their medical

*University Medical Center and Magnuson Health Sciences Center*

*University Medical Center and Magnuson Health Sciences Center*

school has established in the relatively short number of years of its existence and the several Nobel Prize winners associated with it.

Architecturally, the Medical Center to the east and the Health
Sciences Center to the west have been the work of a number of architects.
Nor do the completion dates realistically demonstrate the flux of phases
that have incrementally shaped it. One might be justified in claiming that
this is a project that has no completion date. The first units were completed
in 1948, followed in 1949 by a second phase. Thereafter were successive
construction phases through the 1950s and 1960s, which established the
basic facilities of the Medical and Health Sciences Centers. Further construction moved both east and west, with funding coming from various university, state, federal, and private sources. Initially there was some effort
toward consistency in design, but over the years new construction has
reflected changes in the design language of the profession. An extensive
Health Sciences Libraries and Information Center is one of the wide range
of facilities found here in the service of the medical professions. The newest
addition is the recently completed "K" Wing Biomedical Sciences Research
Building, whose construction was assisted by a $12 million grant from
Microsoft by Bill Gates, its CEO. Its orderly modular facades with their
pattern of windows and tiled wall surfaces and a sequence of steps leading
to a sunlit terrace opening to views of Portage Bay handsomely conclude
the Center's west end. The landscape architect was Swift & Company.
Recently relocated to the southwest corner of this terrace is Robert Maki's
steel plate sculpture. Such terraces, both here and elsewhere on this Walk,

reflect efforts by the university to relieve the otherwise high-density development of this part of the campus.

Dudley Pratt, the sculptor who did some of the work on buildings of the central campus, also did some early terra cotta sculptured inserts for the Medical Center, including a large one on the wall at the northwest corner of "A" Wing as well as several pieces in the former main lobby. Income from the entry area's coffee shop has paid for an extensive art collection in these easily accessed ground floor public spaces, including such visual diversions as Dale Chihuly glass and a variety of paintings and sculpture. Particularly intriguing is a Patrick Zentz sculpture, Stetho, an assemblage of tubes, cylinder, and tuning forks, which emits sounds when activated by people moving through the atrium where it hangs. From this level note also an earth sculpture by Mary Miss in the grounds south of the building, composed of bricked walks, a pergola, fences, water, and lawns with a surrounding ring of evergreen trees.

### 103. Center on Human Development and Disability

*Arnold D. Gangnes, 1969*

The band of development south of the medical center paralleling the shoreline is crowded with a rash of construction, housing mostly water-related programs. This center, however, the most easterly of the group, is more properly seen as lying within the sphere of the university's health sciences

*Center on Human Development and Disability*

commitments. It is composed of three separate but interconnected buildings, all designed by the same architect and built at the same time, though
the four-story unit appears quite different from the others. It houses the
bulk of the Center's research, clinical, and administrative facilities as well as
the Virginia Merrill Bloedel Hearing Research Center. The other two buildings, residentially scaled and low-rise, are designed to serve the experimental and educational needs of the program. They open pleasantly to the
water, creating a reassuring environment for its young patients.

## 104. Fisheries Research Institute

*Young and Richardson, 1951; Ralph Anderson, 1968*

*Fisheries Research Institute*

A unit of the College of Ocean and
Fishery Sciences, the institute's 1950s
building is conventionally uninspired,
but its later east wing by Ralph
Anderson has been much admired for
its imaginative use of red brick, inter-
estingly corbeled to create curved surfaces for the roof cornice, and its
"fisheye" windows angled out to cap-
ture views of Portage Bay. As one
observer noted, "It is a far cry from the
boxlike anonymity of the now out-
dated Bauhaus or international style."
Nearby, closer to the water, is the
Salmon Homing Pond, which has its
own school of Pacific salmon with a
run of several thousand fish that
return home on schedule to the pond
and its auxiliary tanks. Important for instruction and research, the pond
complex is also a popular visitor destination.

## 105. Oceanography Building   *John Graham, 1932*

On this Walk, which focuses on buildings almost entirely modern in design,
this is one of the only two that have design links with central campus's earlier Collegiate Gothic tradition. With a picturesque asymmetrical waterfront
facade and materials and details familiar to the upper campus, the
Oceanography Building would likely have felt more at home there. The

Rockefeller Foundation gave the funds for its construction, an especially welcome gesture given the Depression date in which the building was erected. The school of oceanography's program of chemical oceanographic research is housed here.

*Oceanography Building*

### 106. South Campus Center   *Bumgardner Partnership, 1974*

A boldly stated poured-concrete building, the South Campus Center somewhat dominates its diminutive oceanography neighbor. Viewed from the north, the center is to all appearances like a parking structure, but, taking advantage of its south-facing site's topography, it steps down in a succession of stories and terraces opening out to Portage Bay. One terrace adjoins food services for grand al fresco luncheoning. Functionally, what the HUB provides on upper campus, the South Campus Center serves here to the lower campus; beside food services, there are meeting rooms, a bookstore branch, barbershop, and some recreational facilities. Note in an upper lobby the stained glass portrait of George Washington, with its rather enigmatic aphorism. Incidentally, some will remember that the shoreline the center faces was once the site of the university's well-known Showboat Theater. No boat at all but securely anchored to its site on piling, it was one of the

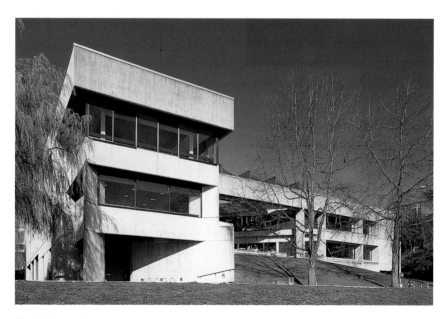

*South Campus Center*

school of drama's theaters featuring student performances. Deterioration and fire code requirements finally led to its destruction in 1994, abetted by the university's commitment toward more friendly waterfront accessibility.

### 107. Harris Hydraulics Laboratory

*Bebb and Gould, 1920; Liddle & Jones, 1960*

Bebb and Gould's only contribution to development on this Walk is this brick building in a Collegiate Gothic style, with brick and terra cotta trim. Its name honors Charles W. Harris, another long-time member of the faculty, who came to the university in 1906 and remained as professor of civil engineering until his retirement in 1951. Its offices and laboratories are

*Harris Hydraulics Laboratory, detail*

used for administration and research in civil engineering and bioengineering. A pleasantly congenial design, the building is substantially obscured by the 1960s modernism of its much later addition.

*Harris Hydraulics Laboratory*

*Marine Sciences Building*

## 108. Marine Sciences Building and Oceanography Teaching Building

**Marine Sciences Building**   *Liddle & Jones, 1967*
**Oceanography Teaching Building**   *Liddle & Jones, 1969*

Both of these water-oriented buildings were designed by the same architect with a similar design vocabulary of poured concrete and metal-clad mansard roofs. They rest on a rather imposing podium—the textured, battered walls faced with river rock. Of the two, the Marine Sciences Building has the immediate waterfront location; its docking area at times accommodates the university navy's flagship, the MV Thomas G. Thompson, a floating oceanography classroom and laboratory administered by the school of oceanography. The 3,05l-ton vessel was commissioned in 1991. When it is docking, its white hull and superstructure bring a glamorous presence to this campus shoreline.

More inland is the Oceanography Teaching Building where the department has classrooms, teaching labs, seminar rooms, and faculty and administrative offices. Here also is where one finds the Fisheries-Oceanography Library.

The university is committed to increasing the visual quality of the

*Oceanography Teaching Building*

shoreline and reinforcing its accessibility as an attractive leisure time and pedestrian campus feature. This has led in recent times to the removal of structures and functions incompatible with that objective—including on this Walk a former surplus Navy ship used for a dormitory and classrooms and the Showboat Theater. As budgets allow, the pace will increasingly be toward realizing and enhancing the unique opportunities the university's waterfront location offers to it and the general community as well.

### 109. Hitchcock Hall  *TRA, 1981*

This Walk ends in the upper west corner of South Campus with Hitchcock Hall. Located at the pedestrian bridge leading to and from the central campus, the brick-clad building is rigorously restrained in design, yet with an elegance of detail that gives it a certain panache over its powerful neighbors. By its location, one might expect it to house some health science-related activity, but instead it is quarters for the department of botany and a nest of other sciences—biochemistry, biology, genetics, and zoology. Professor of Botany C. Leo Hitchcock, for whom the building is named, specialized in plants of the Pacific Northwest, teaching here from 1937 to 1972.

*Hitchcock Hall*

# Southwest Campus

## *Where the Past Meets the Future*

Of all the Walks described in this guide, none draws the visitor more fully into viewing the process of change than this one. This area was of course part of the territorial urban renewal accessions the university had made by the early 1960s. Before that time it had been typically platted with a Seattle street grid of rectangular blocks dominated by the ubiquitous north-south, east-west orientation. Subsequently, over the years a rather scruffy low-density mix of residential and commercial development had emerged, which required full clearance in preparation for the area's new role. How was the university, adorned with the central campus splendors of its monumental plan, to integrate this dowdy adoption—especially that portion south of Pacific Street and west of Fifteenth Avenue? This Walk will reveal the answers to that question.

### 110. Southwest Campus Plan   *Weinstein Copeland Architects and*
*University of Washington, 1994–present*

*Campus viewed from the South*

In the early 1990s the university began the complex process of integrating the southwest campus into the overall design plans of the campus. After months of internal investigations and reports, community meetings, and design reviews, both the university and the city approved the Southwest Campus Plan in 1994. As this Walk will reveal, the implementation of that plan is now underway. The lack of any obvious stylistic constraints on the designers will be evident; each building is examined by the university's architectural commission and landscape advisory committee to satisfy certain design controls, but otherwise designs are judged on their own merits.

The plan called for a major overhaul of the area's street grid. Fifteenth Avenue in particular, starting at the intersection of Pacific Street, was realigned to break the north-south grid and create instead an open space oriented from northeast to southwest—conforming with the orientation of all the space's eastward development south of Pacific Street visited in Walk Ten. Central to the scheme is Portage Bay Vista, and future building and landscaping projects will contribute toward defining its edges. The just completed Ocean Sciences Building is the first to begin that process. The vista is planned to physically and visually join the Physics/Astronomy quad with the Bay and the city beyond—the same design principle that moved the Olmsteds to create Rainier Vista linking the campus with Mt Rainier.

This is the first building whose site plan and form were required to conform to the new Portage Bay Vista; in due course it will be joined by others to establish an architectural frame for both sides of the Vista. The building's sleek glass and metal-clad walls house the dean of the College of Ocean and Fishery Sciences and the laboratories and other facilities supporting oceano-

*Ocean Sciences Building*

graphic research and teaching. Its terrace and entrance lobby open sweepingly to views of Portage Bay and the I-5 bridge.

## 112. Sakuma Viewpoint Park

*McLeod Reckord, landscape architect, 1998*

Although developed well before the Southwest Campus Plan came into effect, the Park fits nicely into it since it contributes to the plan's objective to achieve a higher level of public access to the campus shoreline. This waterfront feature was originally developed in memory of the all too brief professional and teaching career of Professor of Landscape Architecture Donald Sakuma, who died in 1975, having joined the faculty in 1963. Recently rehabilitated with a revised plan, the park continues to invite people to linger there for games of checkers or chess, for lunch, or simply to enjoy views of the waterfront life of Portage Bay.

*Sakuma Viewpoint Park*

## 113. West Campus Parking Garage

*Loschky, Marquardt & Nesholm, 1996*

In consultation with the surrounding residential community, the university has agreed actively to discourage vehicular traffic in the university district and to stabilize the number of parking spaces on campus. This as well as a successful public transit plan has done much to encourage the university population to get out of their cars. The construction of this parking

*West Campus Parking Garage*

garage, therefore, was not to increase the number of campus parking spaces but to compensate for those Southwest Plan parking areas lost in development, to maintain a set number of stalls in the overall campus parking program.

## 114. Academic Computer Center   *Ibsen Nelsen & Associates, 1976*

Just across the street from the parking garage is architectural evidence of the new technology revolution the university is experiencing: the Academic Computer Center. Its entirely poured-concrete exterior and form are weighty

*Academic Computer Center*

testimony to the effects felt on campus in all aspects of its life. "Its no-nonsense concrete form," claimed one critic, "with its ramped bridge to the upper floor and rather stark interiors seems appropriate for tenants and users, mesmerized as they are by the technology of keyboard and screen before them." The center provides its users ranks of computer stations, answers questions on their uses, and provides technical and operational assistance.

### 115. Marine Studies Building

*Streeter Dermanis with Naramore, Bain, Brady & Johanson, 1984*

The Southwest Campus Plan officially continued the policy that shoreline space assignment priority be given to water-oriented facilities; the Marine Studies Building was one of the first whose location was ahead of the Plan but in anticipation of its likely direction. The building in its construction combines both poured-concrete and precast-concrete panels. It houses the school of marine studies, the division of aquaculture and food science, and the Institute for Food Science and Technology. In 1985 a colorful stained glass window by Dick Weiss, *A Sea-Time Story,* by was hung in the lobby.

*Marine Studies Building*

*Fisheries Teaching and Research Center*

## 116. Fisheries Teaching and Research Center
*The Miller/Hull Partnership, 1990*

This later building, constructed a few years after the Marine Studies Building to which it is attached, employs much the same construction technology. Both were precursors of the planning direction that the Southwest Campus Plan was to make official in terms of location and orientation to the site plan. Here one finds classrooms, laboratories, and offices for the school of fisheries.

## 117. Fisheries Building    *Bohlin Cywinski Jackson, 1999*

The third in this triumvirate of sea-oriented facilities is the just completed Fisheries Building, providing classrooms, laboratories, and offices for the school of fisheries. The full-height entrance lobby featuring a staircase to the upper-story levels is dramatized by the floor-to-ceiling windows that face out to the bay. Installed in 2000 is Alexis *Rockman's A Recent History of the World,* a mural based on a map of the world. Also seen from the building is the landscaped garden that lies in the building's angle. Its plan, the work of landscape architect Swift & Company, utilizes the natural swale that crosses the site. Originally the intention had been that the garden design would meld into a salmon homing pond relocated on the nearby Portage Bay shoreline, but for the time being this remains for some future funding.

*Fisheries Building*

*Salmon Homing Pond Near Fisheries Center*

The completion of these three buildings comprises a major chapter in the evolution of the Southwest Campus, as visualized by its 1994 plan. No longer can this corner of the campus be seen as an awkward and neglected adjunct to central campus. It has become instead an increasingly equal participant in the design history of the campus, complementing the vision that the founders had for their University of Washington, "the University of a Thousand Years."

# Bibliography

*A Campus Walk.* Seattle, WA: University Relations, June 1998.

Gates, Charles M. *The First Century at the University of Washington, 1861–1961.* Seattle: University of Washington Press, 1961.

Johnston, Norman J. *The Fountain & the Mountain: The University of Washington Campus 1895–1995.* Woodinville, WA: Documentary Book Publishers Corporation, 1995.

Jones, John Paul. *Campus Plans 1861–1940.* Seattle: University of Washington, 1940.

Ochsner, Karl Jeffrey, ed. *Shaping Seattle Architecture: A Historical Guide to the Architects.* Seattle: University of Washington Press in association with the American Institute of Architects Seattle chapter and the Seattle Architectural Foundation, 1998.

Ojeda, Oscar Riera, ed. *Henry Art Gallery.* Single Building Series Process of an Architectural Work. Gloucester Massachusetts: Rockport Publishers, 1999.

Sale, Roger. *Seattle: Past to Present.* Seattle: University of Washington Press, 1976.

Sanders, Jane. *Into the Second Century: The University of Washington, 1961–1986.* Seattle: University of Washington Press, 1987.

*Southwest Campus Plan.* Seattle: The University of Washington, April 5, 1993.

Talley, Bill. "Ground for Growing: The University of Washington Campus, 1894–1994." *Daily Journal of Commerce* (March 24, 1994).

*Three Quarters of a Century at Washington.* Seattle: University of Washington Alumni Association, 1941.

There was a happy coincidence when the University of Washington was asked by Princeton Architectural Press to participated in a campus guide series featuring outstanding campuses of American universities. For it came at a time when the university's similar but earlier campus publication, *The Fountain and the Mountain* (published in 1995 on the occasion of the hundredth anniversary of the university's occupancy of its present campus), had become somewhat dated by an influx of campus development, most of which had been only marginally acknowledged in 1995 as future campus features, if at all. Thus, when approached to join this select group, the university was pleased to do so and in turn Executive Vice President Weldon E. Ihrig asked me, as author of the earlier book, to undertake the assignment. I accepted with enthusiasm, seeing it as an opportunity to update the published record of our splendid campus and to do so in a mode likely to reach a far larger audience.

Inevitably, much of what one finds in this guide comes from my efforts leading to the 1995 publication. However, for this guide, a different format, to which all in the series conform, is required. More significantly, as already noted, the university campus has in the relatively short span of five years not only completed a number of major new projects on campus, important in themselves, but also has done so in ways that have further enhanced and clarified the remarkable university plan to which they all adhere.

I hope I may therefore be forgiven if I acknowledge that earlier book experience. As I wrote then, "My first memories of the University of Washington, some seventy [five] years ago, were environmental: a row of salmon-pink geraniums topping the wall of the northwest campus that parallels Fifteenth Avenue Northeast. That began a love affair with this campus that is still with me."

In 1995 I noted the assistance received from various colleagues and agencies of the university, whose contributions have now been offered again: Director of Continuing Professional Education Lyn Firkins and Associate Vice President Norman G. Arkans. I want to add for the present record the help of Weldon Ihrig, Susan Smith of the university's Capital Projects Office, Kurt Kiefer, campus art administrator, and my editor at Princeton Architectural Press, Jan Cigliano. A subject attended by so many factual minutiae as this guide is required to incorporate is a sure candidate for error; I take responsibility for them, praying they may be minimal! As for those opinions expressed, I assume that responsibility.

Let me, finally, conclude again with another quote from my past:

"But my richest resource has been the physical evidence of the campus itself: its buildings, its vistas, and its landscape are collective testimony to the commitment and care it has over the years received from those responsible for its nurturing and support. What better observance of the [then] one-hundredth anniversary of the University's move to this wonderful site than to appreciate the magnificent campus around us as we celebrate[d that] historic event."

*Norman J. Johnston*
*Seattle, Washington*

# Index

*(Italics indicate a photograph.)*